Longman Top Pocket Series

D[illegible]
R[illegible]

Longman

Introduction

1. *Techniques of verse*

When asked to define poetry, a modern poet provocatively described it as the stuff written in lines that don't run right to the end of the page. He was suggesting that poetry should not be seen as a purely artificial way of writing which is governed by inflexible rules, and which uses language utterly different from our normal speech and writing. A poet does not have to have flowing locks, think lofty thoughts, or express them in exalted or unnatural language. Yet we must admit that poetry is a rather special form of expression, and does not usually consist merely of prose arranged on the page in a peculiar way. Broadly speaking, verse is distinguished from prose by its greater use of patterned, repeated, or parallel sound and stress, and often by its division into units of identical or similar length.

In speech, we naturally stress some words or syllables more than others. In everyday speech and written prose the stressed elements usually occur at irregular intervals, whereas in verse their occurrence tends to be more or less regular. This pattern of stressed and unstressed elements is *rhythm*. In verse, a systematic repetition of a fixed rhythmical pattern is known as *metre* (see section 6 below).

Metre involves the use of *lines* (see section 7) and, often, of *stanzas* (see section 8). These may be regarded as repeated units of structure which verse uses in addition to the pauses which divide speech into sections of generally irregular length and the sentences and paragraphs which divide most prose.

Repetition of sounds – which is unconscious in our everyday use of language, but more deliberate and emphatic in verse – takes three main forms. *Alliteration* is the repetition of a stressed sound, usually a consonant, at the beginning of two or more words, as in '*w*ailing *w*ind'. *Assonance* is the repetition of a vowel sound in two or more words, as in 'f*i*re and w*i*ne'. *Rhyme* is a repetition of sound at the end of words. Usually the rhyming words appear at the ends of lines of verse, although it is also possible to rhyme a word at the end of a line with one in the middle, to rhyme two words within the same line, or even (not very effectively) to rhyme words at the beginnings of lines.

2. *Definition of rhyme*

Defined more technically, perfect rhyme is the repetition in two or more words of a final stressed vowel sound and of any sounds following it, provided that there are different consonant sounds (or no consonant sound in one case) before that vowel in each word. So *pin* rhymes with *sin*, since the two words have the same vowel sound *i*, the same *n* sound after it, and a different sound before it. *Pin* also rhymes with *in*, which has no sound before the vowel. But *pin* does not truly rhyme with *pen*, which has a different vowel sound, or with *pit* or *pinch*, which have different sounds after the vowel sound.

The rhyming element of a word always begins with a vowel sound. This is a sound which in writing is represented by *a, e, i, o, u,* or occasionally *y*. However, it must be borne in mind that rhyme depends purely on the sound of a word, not on its spelling. Those six letters of the alphabet have to represent at least twenty different vowel sounds in English; the letter *u*, for instance, represents five different vowel sounds in the words *cut, cur, cute, lute,* and *put*.

This dictionary consists of groups of rhyming words, arranged according to the rhyming sound. To avoid the use of difficult methods of indicating sounds, these groups have been arranged in an alphabetical order depending on the most usual spelling of the sound. Hence *tact* appears at **ACT**. Cross-references are given from other common spellings that form the same sound; for example, from *cracked* to **ACT**.

Each group is headed by a word chosen to show the sound of the rhyming part. For example, words with the rhyming sound **aid** (*afraid, blade, brayed,* etc) are headed by the word AFR**AID**, with the rhyming part in bold type. Words in each group are arranged in normal alphabetical order. The headword is not repeated in a group of two or more words when it comes first in alphabetical order.

To avoid needless repetition, some groups of words which the reader can easily deduce are not given here. Regular plural nouns and verb forms ending in *-s* are not shown when the singular noun or basic verb form is shown: so there is an entry for *cure*, but none for *cures*. Similarly, verb forms ending in *-ing* and *-ed* are often omitted, and adverbs formed by adding *-ly* or *-ally* to adjectives are not always given. Such words are usually listed, however, when they rhyme with words which do not appear in the same group as their base form; thus *toes* and plurals of other nouns in the group rhyming with bl**ow** do appear in the group at AR**OSE**.

This small dictionary does not pretend to give an exhaustive list of the countless possible rhymes in English. It contains the words which are likely to be of most value to poets and songwriters, and ensures accurate rhyming.

3. *The use of rhyme*

Rhyme is not an essential part of verse. The ancient Greek and Roman poets used no rhyme, nor did many English poets before the thirteenth century. There have always been some critics objecting to it as artificial and monotonous, or unsuited to certain types of verse (eg long serious poems) and certain subjects.

Rhyme can, however, contribute significant effects to verse. It provides a musical or harmonious element; it can help to give structure and order to a poem; and perfection or ingenuity of rhyming can be sources of satisfaction in themselves.

4. *Types of true rhyme*

Rhymes can be classified according to their length:

(i) a *single* (or *masculine*) rhyme involves a word of one syllable, or the final stressed syllable of a longer word: eg dog–bog, tame–exclaim.

(ii) a *double* (or *feminine*) rhyme involves a word of two syllables, or the last two syllables of a longer word: eg going–flowing, merit–inherit.

(iii) a *triple* rhyme involves a word of three syllables, or the last three syllables of a longer word: eg emulous–tremulous, mendable–dependable.

Rhymes involving more than three syllables are possible, but are rarely used and not included in this dictionary: eg normality–formality, imperialism–materialism.

In rhymes using two or more syllables, one or more of the rhymes may be composed of more than one word: eg habit–grab it, kiss her–miss her. Such rhymes are known as *mosaic* or *composite* rhymes (or occasionally as *Hudibrastic* rhymes); because of their often bizarre quality they are rare in serious poetry but frequent in comic verse. Specimen mosaic rhymes are given at the end of some of the groups in this book, within brackets; users will doubtless think of more.

5. *Other varieties of rhyme*

Many poets have used rhymes which are not true rhymes according to the definition given above. In some cases the reason may be carelessness, or the shortage of true rhymes for a number of common English words; in others, it is a deliberate attempt to produce original effects. Rhymes of these types have not been included in this book, but users may like to experiment with them.

(i) Words which end in the same spelling but not in the same sound, such as dough–cough and blow–brow, are sometimes used as rhymes. These *eye-rhymes* are usually considered defective, but before condemning apparent faults in other poets' use of rhyme one should consider (a) that the poet's pronunciation may differ from one's own, and (b) that English pronunciation has changed over the centuries, and an apparently false rhyme in an old poem may have been perfectly proper in the poet's own time. The sounds on which the rhymes in this dictionary are based are those of 'Received Pronunciation', the standard speech of educated speakers in present-day England. Lack of space makes it impossible to allow for regional and social variants which often might make or mar a rhyme. An American poet might properly rhyme glass with lass; a Londoner could not.

(ii) *Half rhymes* or *para-rhymes* fulfil only partly the conditions of exact rhyming, but two types have been used effectively by some modern poets. *Assonance* involves words which have the same final stressed vowel but different consonant sounds following it (and usually different consonant sounds before it): eg fine–time, stony–holy. *Consonance* (also known as *sour rhyme* or *off rhyme*) involves words which have different final stressed vowels but the same sound following them (and sometimes the same sound before them): eg send–hand, roam–room.

(iii) *Minor-stress rhymes* occur when the rhyming element of one or both words is, in normal use, unstressed or only lightly stressed: eg ring–sowing, tree–weary. Such distortions of normal pronunciation may be amusing in humorous verse, but are generally considered inappropriate to serious verse.

(iv) A true rhyme cannot be made from two words which have exactly the same structure of consonant sound + vowel sound + consonant sound: eg place–displace, moving–unmoving. True rhyme involves difference as well as similarity, but in the case of such pairs (sometimes known as *identities*) there is only similarity.

(v) *Broken rhyme* involves dividing a word at the end of a line. The effect is contrived and usually humorous, although this device has been used by serious poets, as in G M Hopkins' lines

> I caught this morning morning's minion, king-
> dom of daylight's dauphin...
> High there, how he hung upon the rein of a wimpling wing

6. *Metre*

Conventional metre in English verse consists of the repetition of rhythmical units (called *feet*) containing two or three stressed and unstressed syllables in a certain order. In the most important feet, the syllables are arranged as follows:

(i) unstressed + stressed (*iambic* foot). This is the commonest metre in English verse, and tends to produce a regular, rather stately, effect. Thus, marking stressed syllables with a ′ sign, and dividing feet by a vertical line (the end of the foot does not have to come at the end of a word), we can analyse the iambic opening line of Thomas Gray's *Elegy Written in a Country Churchyard* as:

The cúr | few tólls | the knéll | of párt | ing dáy.

(ii) stressed + unstressed (*trochaic* foot). This tends to produce a more rapid motion than iambic metre. For example, from H W Longfellow's *The Song of Hiawatha*:

Shóuld you | aśk me, | whénce these | stóries?

(iii) unstressed + unstressed + stressed (*anapaestic* foot). A leaping or galloping effect is characteristic of this metre. For example, from Lord Byron's *The Destruction of Sennacherib*:

Like the leáves | of the fó | rest when Sú | mmer is gréen.

(iv) stressed + unstressed + unstressed (*dactylic* foot). The general effect is commonly of swift movement. For example, from Lord Tennyson's *The Charge of the Light Brigade*:

Cańnon to | riǵht of them,
Cańnon to | léft of them.

Absolute regularity of metre is difficult to achieve without distorting the usual stresses of pronunciation, and tends to become monotonous in a long poem. The poet's best aim is to establish a basic norm or regular pattern, then to make departures from it by subtle variation – for instance, by introducing a trochaic foot into a basically iambic line. When people say that a line of verse doesn't scan, they mean that the metre undergoes an abrupt, awkward change that we can instinctively recognize even without technical knowledge of metre. This is to be avoided, yet metre need not be as mechanical and inflexible as some accounts of it suggest.

7. *Lines of verse*

Much poetry is written in lines of identical or similar length. Length is usually reckoned by the total number of syllables in a line, although reckoning by the number of stressed syllables only was the practice of many early and some modern poets. Variations in length, even the alternation of short and long lines, are of course perfectly valid, particularly when they occur in a regular fashion.

The technical terms often used to describe the length of a line are somewhat confusing. Counting purely by syllables, a line may be described as, for example, an *octosyllable* (eight syllables), a *decasyllable* (ten syllables), or an *Alexandrine* (a line of twelve syllables, usually forming six iambic feet, often with a distinct pause after the third foot). Or it may be described in terms of the number of feet it contains: hence a *pentameter* has five feet, a *hexameter* has six feet. But since a foot may have two or three syllables, more precise terms must often be used: for example, *iambic pentameter*, which denotes a line of five iambic feet, giving ten syllables.

8. *Stanza forms*

A group of lines in a poem is known as a *stanza* (the term *verse* is sometimes used, but is better avoided because of its other meanings). Stanzas can be of any length and design, and need not be regular; but certain types of stanza, involving fixed patterns of rhyme, metre, and line-length, are so well-established in English poetry that they deserve to be described here.

(i) A stanza of two lines is known as a *couplet*. The lines may be of any length, but an especially common form consists of two rhyming iambic pentameters, called a *heroic couplet*:

Great wits are sure to madness near allied,
And thin partitions do their bounds divide. (John Dryden)

(ii) Stanzas of three lines are generally known as *triplets* or *tercets*. A special form is the *terza rima*, usually with ten syllables to each line, with rhymes linking one stanza to the next. Thus, if we mark the first rhyme 'a', the second 'b', and so on, the rhyme-scheme can be shown as aba–bcb–cdc–ded, etc.

(iii) Stanzas of four lines are called *quatrains*. Various rhyme-schemes are used: abab (often known as the *elegiac stanza*), abcb (*ballad metre*), abba (the *In Memoriam stanza*), or aaba (the *Rubaiyat stanza*). The *Clerihew* is a special type of independent quatrain: a humorous, mainly nonsensical poem about a (usually) famous person. The first line consists of, or at least ends with, the person's name; the lines are of uneven length; the rhyme-scheme is aabb; the sheer silliness is an essential ingredient. For example:

Sir Humphry Davy
Abominated gravy.
He lived in the odium
Of having discovered sodium.

(iv) Stanzas of five lines are *cinquains* or *quintains*. A very well-known type is the *limerick*: a humorous poem, rhyming aabba, with two stresses in the third and fourth lines and three in the others. The first line often ends with the name of a place; the last line may wholly or partly repeat the first:

There was a young woman of Venice
Who thrashed all opponents at tennis;
Her serves were so fast
They caught fire and whizzed past,
And her lobs were an absolute menace.

(v) Six-line stanzas are known as *sestets*. Many different rhyme-schemes are possible: eg ababcc, aaabab.
(vi) Stanzas of seven lines are *septets*. One special form particularly favoured in medieval and Renaissance times was *rhyme royal*, in iambic pentameters rhyming ababbcc.
(vii) Eight-line stanzas are *octets*. A favourite special form is *ottava rima*, usually in iambic pentameters, rhyming abababcc.
(viii) The best-known nine-line stanza is the *Spenserian stanza*, with eight lines of iambic pentameter followed by an Alexandrine, rhyming ababbcbcc.
(ix) One of the commonest stanza forms is the *sonnet*, comprising fourteen lines, usually in iambic pentameter. Many variations of it have been developed, but two particular versions are prevalent. The *Petrarchan* (or *Italian*) *sonnet* consists of an octet, nearly always rhyming abbaabba, and a sestet usually rhyming cdecde or cdcdcd. There is usually a break in thought at the end of the eighth line. The *Shakespearean* (or *English*) *sonnet* is less complex in form, consisting of three quatrains and a couplet, rhyming ababcdcdefefgg.
(x) Many other set forms exist. Most demand intricate rhyming and, often, repetition of whole lines; and although they can produce fine effects, their difficulty and artificiality has made them generally unfavoured in modern times. Some of the better-known ones are:

the *rondelet*: seven lines, of which the first is repeated as the third and seventh. Thus, if we mark repeated lines by a capital letter, the scheme is AbAabbA.

the *rondel*: fourteen lines, of which the first is repeated as the seventh and thirteenth, and the second as the eighth and fourteenth. Thus the scheme is ABbaabABabbaAB.

the *triolet*: eight lines, with the first repeated as the fourth and seventh, and the second as the eighth. Thus: ABaAabAB.

the *rondeau*: this usually has fifteen lines, divided into three stanzas. The opening words of the first line recur as the ninth and fifteenth lines, and the scheme is: aabbaaabbaabbab.

A

BR**A**
see AJ**AR**

BL**AB**
cab
crab
dab
drab
flab
gab
grab
jab
lab
nab
scab
slab
stab
tab

SW**AB**
see BL**OB**

ABBEY
cabby
flabby
gabby
scabby
shabby
tabby

B**ABBLE**
dabble
gabble
rabble
scrabble

H**ABIT**
inhabit
rabbit
(+ grab it *etc*)

ABLE
Abel
Babel
cable
disable
enable
fable
gable
label
Mabel
sable
stable
table

ABLER
stabler

ABLEST
stablest

L**ABOUR**
caber
labour
neighbour
sabre
tabor

B**ABY**
maybe

ACE
apace
base
bass
brace
case
chase
dace
debase
deface
disgrace
displace
efface
embrace
face
grace
grimace
lace
mace
misplace
pace
place
plaice
race
replace
space
trace

REPL**ACEABLE**
traceable

BR**ACED**
see B**ASED**

R**ACER**
see B**ASER**

ATT**ACH**
see B**ATCH**

ACHE
see AW**AKE**

ACID
placid

GR**ACIOUS**
audacious
capacious
contumacious
efficacious
fallacious
flirtatious
gracious
loquacious
mendacious
ostentatious
perspicacious
pertinacious
pugnacious
spacious
tenacious
vexatious
voracious

ATT**ACK**
back

black
clack
crack
hack
jack
knack
lack
pack
plaque
quack
rack
sac
sack
shack
slack
smack
snack
stack
tack
thwack
track
whack
wrack

ATT**ACKED**
see **ACT**

ATT**ACKER**
backer
blacker
cracker
knacker
lacquer
packer
slacker
smacker
stacker
tracker
whacker
(+ sack her *etc*)

BL**ACKEST**
slackest

BR**ACKET**
jacket
packet
placket
racket
racquet
(+ stack it *etc*)

BL**ACKISH**
brackish

C**ACKLE**
crackle
hackle
shackle
tackle

ATT**ACKS**
axe
backs
blacks
clacks
cracks
flax
hacks
jacks
knacks
lacks
lax
packs
plaques
quacks
racks
relax
sacks
shacks
slacks
smacks

snacks
stacks
tacks
tax
thwacks
tracks
wax
whacks
wracks

BACON
see AWAKEN

ACRE
see BAKER

ACT
abstract
act
attacked
attract
backed
blacked
bract
compact
contract
cracked
detract
distract
enact
exact
extract
fact
hacked
impact
intact
jacked
lacked
packed
quacked
racked
react
retract
sacked
slacked
smacked
stacked
subtract
tacked
tact
tracked
tract
transact
whacked

EXACTEST
practised

GALACTIC
didactic
galactic
syntactic
tactic

PRACTICAL
syntactical
tactical

ACTION
abstraction
attraction
compaction
contraction
detraction
distraction
extraction
faction
fraction
inaction
reaction
retraction
satisfaction

subtraction
traction
transaction

COMP-
ACTNESS
exactness
intactness

ACTOR
abstractor
actor
benefactor
compacter
contractor
detractor
exacter
extractor
factor
protractor
retractor
tractor
(+ smacked her *etc*)

F**ACTORY**
phylactery
refractory
satisfactory

FR**ACTURE**
manufacture

VERN**ACULAR**
Dracula
macula
oracular
spectacular
tentacular
vernacular

S**AD**
add
bad
cad
Chad
clad
dad
fad
gad
glad
had
lad
mad
pad
plaid
sad

W**AD**
see COD

M**ADAM**
Adam
macadam
madam
(+ had 'em *etc*)

GL**ADDEN**
madden
sadden

ADDER
bladder
gladder
ladder
madder
sadder
(+ had a *etc*)

ADDLE
paddle

raddle
saddle
skedaddle
straddle
(+ lad'll *etc*)

W**ADDLE**
see C**ODDLE**

C**ADDY**
daddy
faddy
laddy
paddy
(+ had he *etc*)

BL**ADE**
see AFR**AID**

GR**ADER**
see **AIDER**

B**ADGE**
cadge
fadge
Madge

B**ADGER**
cadger

CR**ADLE**
ladle
(+ trade'll *etc*)

B**ADLY**
gladly
madly
sadly

B**ADNESS**
gladness
madness
sadness

CH**AFE**
Ralph
safe
strafe
vouchsafe
waif

S**AFER**
chafer
wafer

CH**AFF**
gaff
giraffe
naff

TR**AFFIC**
see GR**APHIC**

B**AFFLE**
raffle
snaffle
yaffle

CR**AFT**
aft
craft
daft
draft
draught
graft
haft
laughed
raft
scarfed
shaft
staffed

AFTER
dafter
drafter
grafter
laughter
rafter

B**AG**
brag
crag
drag
fag
flag
gag
hag
lag
nag
rag
sag
shag
slag
snag
stag
swag
tag
wag

AGE
assuage
cage
engage
enrage
gage
gauge
page
rage
sage
stage
wage

W**AGER**
gauger
major
stager
wager

J**AGGED**
ragged

J**AGGEDLY**
raggedly

D**AGGER**
dragger
nagger
stagger
swagger
(+ gag her *etc*)

ST**AGGERED**
haggard
laggard
staggered
swaggered

DR**AGGLE**
gaggle
haggle
straggle
waggle
(+ bag'll *etc*)

M**AGIC**
tragic

M**AGICAL**
tragical

AGILE
fragile

DRAGON
flagon
waggon

FLAGRANT
fragrant
vagrant

PLAGUE
Haig
vague

AFRAID
aid
allayed
bayed
betrayed
blade
braid
brayed
brigade
conveyed
crusade
decayed
delayed
dismayed
disobeyed
displayed
fade
flayed
frayed
glade
grade
grenade
homemade
invade
jade
laid
lemonade
made
maid
masquerade
mislaid
neighed
obeyed
paid
parade
persuade
played
portrayed
prayed
preyed
raid
repaid
shade
spade
sprayed
staid
stayed
strayed
suede
surveyed
swayed
trade
wade
waylaid
weighed

SAID
see AHEAD

AIDER
Ada
crusader
grader
invader
masquerader
persuader
raider
trader
wader

WAIF
see CHAFE

FRAIL
ail
ale
assail
bail
bale
Braille
dale
exhale
fail
flail
frail
gale
gaol
hail
hale
impale
inhale
jail
kale
mail
male
nail
pail
pale
quail
rail
sail
sale
scale
shale
snail
stale
tail
tale
trail
vale
veil
wail
whale
Yale

FRAILER
bailer
gaoler
hailer
haler
paler
railer
sailor
scalar
scaler
staler
tailor
trailer
Venezuela
wailer
whaler

FRAILEST
halest
palest
stalest

DAILY
Bailey
daily
gaily
Israeli
ukulele

AIM
acclaim
aim
became
blame
came
claim

dame
declaim
disclaim
exclaim
fame
flame
frame
game
lame
maim
name
proclaim
reclaim
same
shame
tame

DISCL**AIMER**
see G**AMER**

AG**AIN**
abstain
again
Bahrain
bane
blain
brain
campaign
cane
chain
champagne
complain
contain
crane
Dane
deign
detain
drain
entertain
explain
fain
feign
gain
grain
humane
inane
insane
Jane
lain
lane
main
maintain
mane
obtain
ordain
pain
pane
plain
plane
profane
rain
refrain
regain
reign
rein
remain
restrain
retain
sane
slain
Spain
sprain
stain
strain
sustain
swain
train
urbane
vain
vane

vein
wane

ATT**AINABLE**
gainable
maintainable
obtainable
sustainable
trainable

CONT**AINER**
abstainer
campaigner
complainer
container
entertainer
explainer
gainer
humaner
inaner
insaner
maintainer
obtainer
plainer
planer
profaner
retainer
saner
strainer
trainer
vainer

PL**AINEST**
see HUM**ANEST**

M**AINLY**
see INS**ANELY**

F**AINT**
ain't
complaint
constraint
faint
feint
paint
plaint
quaint
restraint
saint
taint

F**AINTER**
painter
quainter

F**AINTEST**
quaintest

F**AINTLY**
quaintly
saintly

F**AINTNESS**
quaintness

AFF**AIR**
air
aware
Ayr
bare
bear
beware
blare
care
chair
Clare
compare
dare
declare
despair
elsewhere
ere

fair
fare
flair
flare
forbear
glare
hair
hare
heir
impair
lair
laissez-faire
mare
mayor
millionaire
pair
pare
pear
prayer
prepare
rare
repair
scare
share
snare
spare
square
stair
stare
swear
tear
their
there
wear
where

REPAIRABLE
bearable
declarable
repairable
shareable
wearable

FAIRER
bearer
declarer
fairer
rarer
repairer
Sarah
scarer
sharer
sparer
squarer
wearer

FAIREST
see BAREST

AIRIER
Bulgaria
charier
hairier
scarier
warier

AIRIEST
chariest
hairiest
scariest
wariest

AIRILY
charily
scarily
warily

AIRINESS
chariness

hairiness
wariness

FAIRLY
see BARELY

FAIRNESS
see AWARENESS

AFFAIRS
airs
bares
bears
blares
cares
chairs
compares
dares
declares
despairs
downstairs
fairs
fares
flairs
flares
forbears
glares
hairs
hares
heirs
impairs
lairs
mares
mayors
millionaires
pairs
pares
pears
prayers
prepares
repairs
scares
shares
snares
spares
squares
stairs
stares
swears
tears
theirs
unawares
upstairs
wears

AIRY
see VARY

RAISE
see MAZE

DAISY
see CRAZY

WAIT
see DATE

FAITH
wraith

MAJOR
see WAGER

AWAKE
ache
awake
bake
brake
break
cake
drake
fake

flake
forsake
hake
lake
make
mistake
opaque
overtake
partake
quake
rake
sake
shake
sheik
slake
snake
stake
steak
take
undertake
wake

AW**AKEN**

bacon
forsaken
Jamaican
mistaken
shaken
taken
waken

B**AKER**

acre
baker
breaker
faker
Jamaica
maker
nacre
opaquer
overtaker
Quaker
raker
shaker
taker
undertaker

KH**AKI**

see D**ARKY**

B**ALD**

see APP**ALLED**

PALE(R, ST)

see **FRAIL(ER, EST)**

MOR**ALE**

see SN**ARL**

C**ALF**

giraffe
graph
half
laugh
scarf
staff

REG**ALIA**

Australia
azalea
bacchanalia
dahlia
marginalia
paraphernalia
regalia
saturnalia

IT**ALIC**

Alec

cephalic
Gallic
italic
metallic
phallic
salic

M**ALICE**

Alice
chalice
malice
palace

ACTU**ALITY**

artificiality
banality
brutality
congeniality
cordiality
egality
finality
formality
frugality
hospitality
immortality
legality
liberality
locality
mentality
morality
mortality
municipality
nationality
normality
originality
personality
practicality
principality
rationality
reality
sentimentality
sexuality
speciality
technicality
totality
vitality

T**ALK**

see F**ORK**

ALL

appal
awl
ball
brawl
call
caul
crawl
drawl
enthral
fall
gall
Gaul
hall
haul
install
mall
maul
Nepal
overall
overhaul
pall
Paul
recall
Saul
scrawl
shawl
small
sprawl
squall
stall

tall
thrall
trawl
wall

APP**ALLED**
bald
balled
brawled
called
crawled
drawled
enthralled
galled
hauled
installed
mauled
overhauled
palled
recalled
scald
scrawled
sprawled
squalled
stalled
trawled
walled

C**ALLER**
crawler
faller
installer
mauler
scrawler
smaller
taller
trawler

G**ALLERY**
salary

SM**ALLEST**
tallest

ALLEY
bally
dally
galley
rally
sally
Sally
tally
valley

D**ALLIED**
invalid
pallid
rallied
sallied
tallied
valid

BATT**ALION**
Italian
medallion
rapscallion
stallion

G**ALLON**
Alan
gallon
talon

C**ALLOUS**
callus
Dallas
palace
Pallas
phallus

SW**ALLOW**
see F**OLLOW**

SH**ALLOW**
aloe
callow
fallow
hallow
mallow
sallow
shallow
tallow
(+ shall owe *etc*)

SQU**ALLY**
crawly
scrawly
sprawly

C**ALM**
see **ARM**

C**ALMER**
see **ARMOUR**

ALP
palp
scalp

F**ALSE**
waltz

S**ALT**
assault
default
exalt
fault
halt
malt
salt
vault

ALTER
altar
assaulter
falter
halter
Malta
palter
salter
vaulter

C**ALVE**
see C**ARVE**

S**ALVE**
valve

AN**ALYSIS**
catalysis
dialysis
paralysis

AM
clam
cram
dam
damn
dram
gram
ham
jam
jamb
lam
lamb
ma'am
Pam
pram
ram

Sam
scram
sham
slam
swam
tram
yam

AMBER
camber
clamber
mamba
samba

AMBLE
bramble
gamble
gambol
ramble
scamble
scramble
shamble

G**AMBLER**
rambler

C**AME**
see **AIM**

C**AMEL**
enamel
mammal
trammel

G**AMELY**
lamely
namely
tamely

G**AMER**
disclaimer
gamer
lamer
proclaimer
tamer

G**AMEST**
lamest
tamest

EX**AMINE**
famine

M**AMMAL**
see C**AMEL**

H**AMMER**
clamour
crammer
enamour
glamour
grammar
hammer
jammer
slammer
stammer
yammer

G**AMMON**
mammon
salmon

C**AMP**
amp
champ
clamp
cramp
damp
gamp
lamp

ramp
scamp
stamp
tamp
tramp
vamp

SWAMP
see **POMP**

CAMPER
damper
hamper
pamper
scamper
tamper

AMPLE
trample

EXAMPLE
sample

BAN
an
Ann(e)
ban
began
bran
can
clan
Dan
fan
flan
Jan
Japan
man
Milan
pan
plan
ran
scan
span
tan
than
van

ADVANCE
askance
chance
dance
enhance
entrance (verb)
France
glance
lance
prance
stance
trance

ROMANCE
see **EXPANSE**

ADVANCER
answer
dancer
lancer
prancer

BLANCH
branch
ranch

ANCHOR
see **BANKER**

FANCY
geomancy
Nancy
necromancy

AND
band
banned
bland
brand
canned
disband
expand
fanned
gland
grand
hand
inland
land
manned
misunderstand
panned
planned
sand
scanned
secondhand
spanned
stand
strand
tanned
understand
withstand

COMM**AND**
darned
demand
yarned

W**AND**
see BEY**OND**

P**ANDA**
Amanda
blander
expander
gander
grander
memoranda
Miranda
panda
pander
propaganda
Uganda
veranda

EXP**ANDABLE**
understandable

B**ANDED**
branded
candid
candied
disbanded
expanded
handed
landed
sanded
stranded
(+ Ann did *etc*)

COMM**ANDER**
demander
slander

W**ANDER**
see ABSC**ONDER**

GR**ANDEST**
blandest
propagandist

C**ANDLE**
dandle
handle
Randall
sandal

scandal
vandal

HANDSOME
ransom
transom

BRANDY
Andy
bandy
brandy
candy
dandy
handy
sandy
shandy

BANE
see AGAIN

PANEL
see CHANNEL

INSANELY
inanely
insanely
mainly
plainly
profanely
sanely
urbanely
vainly

MISCELL-ANEOUS
contempor-aneous
instantaneous
miscellaneous
simultaneous
spontaneous

MISCELL-ANEOUSLY
contempor-aneously
instantaneously
miscellaneously
simultaneously
spontaneously

HUMANEST
inanest
insanest
plainest
profanest
sanest
urbanest
vainest

PLANET
see GRANITE

BANG
clang
fang
gang
hang
harangue
pang
rang
sang
slang
sprang
tang
twang

ARRANGE
change
derange
estrange

exchange
grange
mange
range
strange

ARR**ANGER**
changer
danger
exchanger
ranger
stranger
(+ change her *etc*)

B**ANGER**
clanger
clangour
ganger
hangar
hanger
(+ sang a *etc*)

ANGLE
bangle
dangle
entangle
jangle
mangle
spangle
strangle
tangle
wangle
wrangle

ANGUISH
languish

M**ANIA**
Albania
Lithuania
mania
Pennsylvania
Romania
Tasmania
zanier

MECH**ANIC**
manic
organic
panic
satanic
titanic
volcanic

SP**ANIEL**
Daniel
Nathaniel
spaniel

B**ANISH**
clannish
mannish
Spanish
vanish

GR**ANITE**
gannet
granite
Janet
planet
(+ ban it *etc*)

CHRISTI**ANITY**
humanity
inanity
insanity
profanity
sanity
urbanity
vanity

CRANIUM
geranium
titanium
uranium

BANK
blank
clank
crank
dank
drank
flank
frank
hank
lank
plank
prank
rank
sank
shank
shrank
spank
stank
tank
thank
yank

BANKER
anchor
blanker
canker
chancre
danker
flanker
franker
lanker
rancour
ranker
tanker

BLANKEST
dankest
frankest
lankest
rankest

BLANKLY
dankly
frankly
lankly
rankly

MANLY
Stanley

BANNED
see AND

CHANNEL
annal
channel
flannel
panel

BANNER
Anna
manner
manor
planner
scanner
spanner
tanner

CLANNISH
see BANISH

ANNUAL
manual

ANNUALLY
manually

CANNY
Annie
canny
Danny
Fanny
granny
nanny
uncanny

MANOR
see **BANNER**

EXPANSE
manse
romance
stance

RANSOM
see **HANDSOME**

ANSWER
see **ADVANCER**

ANT
cant
extant
pant
rant
recant
scant

GRANT
aren't
aunt
can't
chant
enchant
grant
plant
shan't
slant
transplant

ANTIC
frantic
gigantic
pedantic
romantic
semantic
sycophantic
transatlantic

MANUAL
see **ANNUAL**

ANY
see **PENNY**

CAP
chap
clap
flap
gap
hap
lap
map
nap
overlap
pap
rap
sap
scrap
slap
snap
strap
tap
trap
wrap
yap

APE
agape

ape
cape
crepe
drape
escape
gape
grape
jape
nape
rape
scrape
shape
tape

CH**APEL**
see **APPLE**

C**APER**
draper
escaper
gaper
paper
scraper
shaper
taper
vapour

DR**APERY**
napery
papery
vapoury

GR**APHIC**
seraphic
telegraphic
traffic

P**APIST**
rapist

M**APLE**
papal
staple

APPLE
chapel
dapple
grapple

C**APS**
apse
chaps
claps
collapse
elapse
flaps
gaps
laps
lapse
maps
naps
overlaps
perhaps
raps
relapse
saps
scraps
slaps
snaps
straps
taps
traps
wraps
yaps

AD**APT**
apt
capped
clapped
flapped
lapped

mapped
napped
overlapped
rapped
rapt
sapped
scrapped
slapped
snapped
strapped
tapped
trapped
wrapped
yapped

AD**APTER**
captor
chapter

AJ**AR**
are
bar
bazaar
bra
car
catarrh
char
cigar
debar
far
guitar
hussar
jar
ma
mar
pa
par
scar
shah
spa
spar
star
tar
tsar

W**AR**
see AD**ORE**

DISP**ARAGE**
see C**ARRIAGE**

COMP**ARATIVE**
declarative
narrative
preparative

B**ARB**
garb

B**ARBER**
arbour
harbour

M**ARBLE**
barbel
garble
marble

P**ARCEL**
see C**ASTLE**

ARCH
larch
march
parch
starch

ARCHER
marcher

CARD
bard
barred
bombard
card
chard
charred
guard
hard
jarred
lard
marred
nard
pard
regard
retard
scarred
shard
sparred
starred
tarred
yard

WARD
see CORD

GARDEN
harden
pardon

WARDEN
see CORDON

HARDER
ardour
carder
guarder
harder
larder

BARE
see AFFAIR

BARELY
fairly
rarely
squarely

AWARENESS
bareness
fairness
rareness
spareness
squareness

BAREST
fairest
rarest
sparest
squarest

SCARF
see CALF

DWARF
wharf

BARGE
charge
discharge
enlarge
large
marge
raj
sarge

CARGO
argot
cargo

Chicago
embargo
Fargo
largo

BARBARIAN
agrarian
antiquarian
Aryan
barbarian
Bavarian
Bulgarian
Caesarean
centenarian
disciplinarian
grammarian
Hungarian
humanitarian
librarian
millenarian
parliamentarian
riparian
vegetarian
vulgarian

ARID
see CARRIED

WARIEST
see AIRIEST

CHARIOT
Harriet
Iscariot
lariat
Marriott

PRECARIOUS
gregarious
hilarious
multifarious
nefarious
various
vicarious

CHARITY
barbarity
charity
clarity
familiarity
irregularity
parity
peculiarity
popularity
similarity
singularity
solidarity
vulgarity

BARK
arc
ark
bark
barque
clerk
dark
embark
hark
Iraq
lark
mark
nark
park
remark
shark
spark
stark

DARKER
barker
marker
parka

parker
starker

DARKY
khaki
parky
sake (= Japanese drink)

SNARL
Carl
dhal
marl
morale
snarl

SNARLED
gnarled

BARLEY
Charlie
marly
parley

DARLING
snarling
starling

ALARM
arm
balm
barm
calm
charm
embalm
farm
harm
ma'm
palm
psalm
qualm
smarm

WARM(ER)
see FORM(ER)

ARMLESS
charmless
harmless

ARMOUR
calmer
charmer
drama
embalmer
farmer
palmer
panorama
pyjama

BARN
darn
Iran
Pakistan
Sudan
tarn
yarn

DARNED
see COMMAND

GARNER
darner
garner
Ghana
gymkhana

GARNISH
tarnish
varnish

HARP
carp
scarp
sharp

EMB**ARRASS**
arras
harass

B**ARRED**
see C**ARD**

B**ARREL**
apparel
barrel
carol

C**ARRIAGE**
disparage
garage
marriage

C**ARRIED**
arid
harried
married
parried
tarried

C**ARRION**
clarion
Marian

C**ARROT**
Barrett
carat
carrot
claret
garret
parrot

ARROW
barrow
farrow
harrow
marrow
narrow
sparrow
tarot
yarrow

C**ARRY**
Barry
Gary
harry
Harry
Larry
marry
parry
tarry

B**ARS**
bazaars
bras
cars
chars
cigars
guitars
hussars
jars
mars
Mars
scars
shahs
spas
spars
stars
tars
tsars
vase

SPARSE
see **BRASS**

HARSH
marsh
moustache

ARSON
Carson
fasten
parson

APART
art
cart
chart
dart
depart
fart
hart
heart
mart
part
smart
start
tart

BARTER
carter
charter
darter
garter
martyr
smarter
starter
Tartar
tarter

FARTHER
see **FATHER**

IMPARTIAL
marshal
martial
partial

ARTICLE
particle

ARTISAN
bartizan
partisan

ARTIST
Chartist
smartest
tartest

PARTLY
smartly
tartly

CARTON
hearten
smarten
tartan

ARTY
hearty
party
smarty
tarty

CARVE
calve
halve
starve

VARY
airy

canary
chary
contrary
dairy
fairy
hairy
Mary
prairie
scary
vary
wary

AS
has
jazz
razz
whereas

FASCINATE
see
ASS**ASSINATE**

ERASE
see M**AZE**

BASE
see **ACE**

BASED
baste
braced
cased
chased
chaste
debased
defaced
disgraced
displaced
effaced
embraced
faced
graced
grimaced
haste
laced
misplaced
paced
paste
placed
raced
replaced
spaced
taste
traced
waist
waste

BASER
baser
bracer
chaser
debaser
defacer
embracer
grimacer
pacer
placer
racer
spacer
tracer

ASH
abash
bash
brash
cache
cash
clash
crash
dash
flash

gash
gnash
hash
lash
mash
plash
rash
sash
slash
smash
splash
thrash
trash

W**ASH**
see G**OSH**

CR**ASHER**
basher
brasher
clasher
flasher
haberdasher
masher
rasher
slasher
smasher
splasher
thrasher

BR**ASHEST**
flashest
rashest

F**ASHION**
ashen
compassion
fashion
passion
ration

B**ASIN**
chasten
hasten
Jason
mason

INV**ASION**
Asian
occasion
persuasion

ASK
bask
Basque
cask
flask
mask
masque
task

CH**ASM**
plasm
spasm

CL**ASP**
gasp
grasp
hasp
rasp

BR**ASS**
class
farce
glass
grass
pass
sparse
surpass

LASS
ass
bass
crass
crevasse
gas
lass
mass

BASS
see **ACE**

CLASSED
see **FAST**

CLASSIFY
gasify
pacify

ASSASSINATE
deracinate
fascinate

PASSION
see **FASHION**

MASSIVE
impassive
massive
passive

MASSIVELY
impassively
massively
passively

FAST
aghast
blast
cast
caste
classed
contrast
fast
grassed
last
mast
passed
past
surpassed
vast

TASTE
see **BASED**

TASTEFUL
wasteful

TASTEFULLY
wastefully

HASTEN
see **BASIN**

FASTEN
see **ARSON**

BROADCASTER
caster
castor
disaster
faster
headmaster
master
pastor
plaster
vaster

FASTEST
vastest

DRASTIC
bombastic
elastic
enthusiastic
fantastic
gymnastic
iconoclastic
mastic
plastic
sarcastic
spastic

HASTIER
pastier
tastier

HASTIEST
pastiest
tastiest

HASTILY
tastily

CASTLE
parcel

HASTY
pasty
tasty

AT
bat
brat
cat
chat
combat
drat
fat
flat
gnat
hat
mat
matt
pat
plait
rat
sat
slat
spat
that
vat

WHAT
see BLOT

DATABLE
debatable
inflatable
locatable
translatable
statable

BATCH
attach
batch
catch
despatch
detach
dispatch
hatch
latch
match
patch
scratch
snatch
thatch

WATCH
see NOTCH

SCRATCHER
catcher
snatcher
stature

HATCHET
latchet
ratchet
(+ catch it *etc*)

DATE
abate
abdicate
aggravate
agitate
annotate
ate
await
bait
bate
captivate
castrate
collate
crate
create
cremate
date
debate
dictate
dilate
donate
eight
elate
estate
fate
frustrate
gait
gate
grate
great
hate
inflate
innate
irate
Kate
Kuwait
late
locate
mate
migrate
narrate
overweight
pate
plate
postdate
prate
prostrate
rate
relate
rotate
sate
sedate
skate
slate
spate
state
straight
strait
translate
understate
up-to-date
vacate
vibrate
wait
weight

ATE
see NET

FATEFUL
grateful
hateful

LATELY
greatly
innately
irately
lately
prostrately
sedately
stately
straightly
straitly

ABATEMENT
statement
understatement

LATENESS
greatness
innateness
irateness
lateness
sedateness
straightness
straitness

PATENT
blatant
latent
patent

LATER
abater
abdicator
agitator
annotator
baiter
cater
collater
crater
creator
data
dater
debater
dictator
dilator
donator
grater
greater
hater
inflator
later
locater
migrator
narrator
pater
plater
relater
skater
slater
spectator
straighter
straiter
traitor
translator
vibrator
waiter

WATER
see **PORTER**

LATEST
greatest
latest
straightest
straitest

BATH
Garth

hearth
path

BATHE
lathe
scathe
spathe
swathe

F**ATHER**
farther
father
rather

ACROB**ATIC**
aquatic
aristocratic
aromatic
Asiatic
attic
automatic
bureaucratic
democratic
diplomatic
dramatic
emphatic
erratic
mathematic
melodramatic
operatic
pneumatic
problematic
static
systematic
traumatic

L**ATIN**
satin
(+ cat in *etc*)

N**ATION**
abdication
accommodation
admiration
aggravation
agitation
amputation
annotation
anticipation
application
appreciation
assassination
association
aviation
calculation
castration
celebration
circulation
civilization
collation
combination
communication
compensation
confiscation
congratulation
congregation
conservation
consideration
conversation
cooperation
creation
cremation
cultivation
declaration
decoration
destination
deterioration
determination
dictation
dilation
domination

donation
duplication
education
elation
elimination
estimation
examination
explanation
foundation
frustration
generation
hallucination
identification
illumination
illustration
imagination
imitation
immigration
incorporation
indication
indoctrination
inflation
information
inspiration
interpretation
interrogation
intimidation

invitation
isolation
legislation
liberation
location
lubrication
migration
ministration
miscalculation
multiplication
narration
nation
notification
obliteration
occupation
operation
oration
organization
penetration
perspiration
plantation
population
premeditation
preparation
presentation
proclamation
pronunciation

prostration
provocation
publication
punctuation
purgation
qualification
radiation
recreation
regulation
relation
relegation
representation
reputation
reservation
resignation
revelation
rotation
satiation
salvation
sedation
sensation
separation
situation
speculation
station
stimulation
stipulation

suffocation
taxation
temptation
termination
transformation
translation
vacation
vaccination
variation
vegetation
ventilation
vibration
violation
vocation

CONGREG-
ATIONAL
conversational
educational
inspirational
occupational
operational
recreational
representational
sensational

OSTENT-
ATIOUS
see GR**ACIOUS**

L**ATITUDE**
attitude
beatitude
gratitude
ingratitude
latitude
platitude

F**ATNESS**
flatness
patness

M**ATRON**
natron
patron

B**ATTER**
chatter
clatter
fatter
flatter
hatter
latter
matter
natter
patter
platter
scatter
shatter
smatter
splatter
tatter
(+ at her *etc*)

CH**ATTERER**
flatterer
scatterer

P**ATTERN**
baton
fatten
flatten
pattern
Saturn
slattern

B**ATTERY**
cattery
flattery

F**ATTEST**
flattest
pattest

B**ATTLE**
cattle
chattle
prattle
rattle
Seattle
tattle
(+ that'll *etc*)

ST**ATURE**
see SCR**ATCHER**

APPAR**ATUS**
efflatus
hiatus
status

SL**ATY**
see **EIGHTY**

DEB**AUCH**
see P**ORCH**

FR**AUD**
see C**ORD**

L**AUGH**
see H**ALF**

L**AUGHED**
see CR**AFT**

C**AUGHT**
see F**ORT**

D**AUGHTER**
see P**ORTER**

L**AUGHTER**
see **AFTER**

N**AUGHTY**
see F**ORTY**

M**AUL**
see **ALL**

F**AULT**
see S**ALT**

H**AUNCH**
launch
paunch
stanch
staunch

D**AUNT**
gaunt
haunt
jaunt
taunt
vaunt

AUNT
see GR**ANT**

C**AUSE**
see AD**ORES**

C**AUTION**
see AB**ORTION**

AUTUMN
postmortem
(+ caught 'em
etc)

BEH**AVE**
brave
cave
crave
Dave
deprave
engrave
forgave
gave
grave
knave
lave
misbehave
nave
pave
rave
save
shave
slave
stave
they've
waive
wave

GR**AVEL**
cavil
gavel
gravel
ravel
travel
unravel

BR**AVELY**
gravely

H**AVEN**
Avon
craven
graven
haven
shaven

BR**AVER**
caver
engraver
favour
flavour
graver
laver
paver
quaver
raver
saver
shaver
slaver
waiver
waver

C**AVERN**
tavern

BR**AVEST**
gravest

BEH**AVIOUR**
pavior
saviour

GR**AVY**
cavy
Davy
gravy
navy
wavy

DR**AW(S)**
see AD**ORE(s)**

B**AWDRY**
Audrey
tawdry

CLAWED
see **CORD**

AWFUL
lawful

AWFULLY
lawfully

HAWK
see **FORK**

HAWKER
corker
gawker
porker
stalker
talker
walker

CRAWL
see **ALL**

DAWN
see **ADORN**

GAWP
warp

LAWYER
sawyer
(+ saw yer *etc*)

AXE, **FLAX**
see **ATTACKS**

FLAXEN
Jackson
klaxon
saxon
waxen

WAY
allay
away
bay
betray
bouquet
brae
bray
clay
convey
day
decay
delay
dismay
disobey
display
dray
fay
fey
flay
fray
gay
grey
halfway
hay
jay
lay
Malay
may
midday
midway
mislay
nay
neigh
obey
pay
play
portray

pray
prey
ray
repay
say
slay
sleigh
spray
stay
straightaway
stray
survey
sway
they
today
tray
way
waylay
weigh

M**AYBE**
see B**ABY**

ALL**AYED**
see AFR**AID**

BETR**AYER**
conveyer
gayer
greyer
layer
Malaya
payer
player
sprayer
stayer
surveyor

P**AYMENT**
claimant
defrayment
payment
raiment

D**AYS**
see M**AZE**

M**AZE**
allays
amaze
baize
bays
betrays
blaze
bouquets
braes
brays
braze
clays
conveys
craze
days
daze
decays
delays
dismays
disobeys
displays
drays
erase
flays
frays
gaze
graze
greys
haze
jays
lays
laze
maize

maze
middays
mislays
neighs
obeys
pays
phase
phrase
plays
portrays
praise
prays
preys
raise
rase
rays
raze
repays
slays
sleighs
sprays
stays
strays
surveys
sways
trays
waylays
ways
weighs

BL**AZER**
brazer
eraser
gazer
grazer
laser
phasor
praiser
raiser
razor

CR**AZIER**
hazier
lazier
mazier

CR**AZIEST**
haziest
laziest
maziest

CR**AZILY**
hazily
lazily
mazily

CR**AZY**
daisy
hazy
lazy
mazy

J**AZZ**
see **AS**

E

BE
see AGREE

PEA
see AGREE

PEACE
see CEASE

BEACH
beech
beseech
bleach
breach
breech
each
impeach
leach
leech
overreach
peach
preach
reach
screech
speech
teach

TEACHER
creature
feature
leacher
overreacher
preacher
screecher
teacher

BEACON
deacon
weaken

AHEAD
bed
bled
bread
bred
dead
dread
fed
fled
Fred
head
instead
lead
led
Ned
overhead
pled
read
red
said

shed
shred
sled
sped
spread
stead
Ted
thread
tread
wed

BEAD
see DEED

HEADER
bedder
Cheddar
deader
dreader
header
redder
shredder
sledder
spreader
threader
treader

DEADEST
dreadest
reddest

HEADIER
readier
steadier

HEADIEST
readiest
steadiest

BREADLINE
deadline
headline

DEADLOCK
headlock
wedlock

DEADNESS
redness

ALREADY
eddy
heady
Neddy
ready
steady
Teddy

LEAF
see CHIEF

DEAF
see CHEF

DEAFEST
prefaced

EAGLE
see LEGAL

LEAGUE
see FATIGUE

BEAK
antique
bleak
cheek
clique
creak
creek
freak

Greek
leak
leek
meek
oblique
peak
peek
pique
reek
seek
shriek
sleek
sneak
speak
squeak
streak
teak
technique
tweak
unique
weak
week
wreak

BREAK
see AWAKE

BEAKER
bleaker
eureka
loudspeaker
meeker
obliquer
seeker
sleeker
sneaker
speaker
squeaker
Tanganyika
weaker

BLEAKEST
meekest
sleekest
weakest

BLEAKLY
meekly
obliquely
sleekly
uniquely
weakly
weekly

CREAKY
cheeky
creaky
leaky
reeky
sneaky
squeaky
streaky

APPEAL
conceal
congeal
deal
eel
feel
genteel
heal
heel
he'll
imbecile
keel
kneel
Lille
meal
Neil
ordeal
peal

peel
real
reel
repeal
reveal
seal
she'll
squeal
steal
steel
teal
veal
weal
we'll
wheel
zeal

APP**EALED**
concealed
congealed
field
healed
heeled
keeled
kneeled
peeled
reeled
repealed
revealed
sealed
shield
squealed
steeled
weald
wheeled
wield
yield

APP**EALER**
concealer
dealer
feeler
healer
kneeler
peeler
Sheila
squealer
stealer

APP**EALING**
ceiling
concealing
congealing
dealing
feeling
healing
heeling
kneeling
pealing
peeling
repealing
revealing
sealing
squealing
stealing
steeling
wheeling

D**EALT**
see B**ELT**

H**EALTH**
stealth
wealth

B**EAM**
blaspheme
bream
cream
deem
dream

esteem
extreme
gleam
ream
redeem
scheme
scream
seam
seem
steam
stream
supreme
team
theme

BEAMER
blasphemer
dreamer
femur
gleamer
lemur
reamer
redeemer
schemer
screamer
steamer
streamer

DREAMT
see ATTEMPT

BEAN
see SEEN

HEAP
see ASLEEP

LEAPT
see ACCEPT

BEAR
see AFFAIR

APPEAR
adhere
appear
auctioneer
beer
bier
blear
brigadier
buccaneer
career
cashier
cavalier
cheer
clear
cohere
dear
deer
disappear
domineer
drear
ear
endear
engineer
fear
frontier
gear
hear
here
interfere
jeer
Korea
leer
mere
mountaineer
near
overhear
overseer
peer
persevere

pier
pioneer
queer
rear
revere
sear
seer
severe
shear
sheer
sincere
smear
sneer
souvenir
spear
sphere
steer
tear (noun)
veneer
volunteer
weir
year

APP**EARANCE**
adherence
appearance
clearance
coherence
disappearance
interference
perseverance

S**EARCH**
see CH**URCH**

H**EARD**
see ABS**URD**

APP**EARED**
adhered
beard
bleared
careered
cashiered
cheered
cleared
cohered
disappeared
domineered
endeared
engineered
feared
geared
interfered
jeered
leered
neared
peered
persevered
pioneered
reared
revered
sheared
smeared
sneered
speared
steered
veneered
volunteered
weird

CL**EARER**
chimera
clearer
dearer
era
Madeira
nearer
queerer
severer
sheerer

sincerer
sneerer
Vera

CLEAREST
blearest
dearest
drearest
merest
nearest
queerest
severest
sheerest
sincerest

FEARFUL
cheerful
earful
fearful
tearful

FEARFULLY
cheerfully
fearfully
tearfully

DREARIER
see EXTERIOR

PEARL
see CURL

CLEARLY
dearly
merely
nearly
queerly
really
severely
sincerely
yearly

EARLY
see CURLY

YEARN
see URN

CLEARNESS
dearness
nearness
queerness

HEART
see APART

EARTH
see BIRTH

DREARY
beery
bleary
cheery
deary
dreary
eerie
eyrie
query
smeary
theory
weary

PEASANT
pheasant
pleasant
present
unpleasant

PLEASANTLY
presently
unpleasantly

CEASE
caprice
crease
decease
decrease
fleece
geese
grease
Greece
increase
lease
niece
obese
peace
piece
police
release

EASE
see AGREES

CEASED
see BEAST

EASEL
diesel
measle
teasel
weasel

EASILY
breezily
queasily
uneasily
wheezily

EASINESS
breeziness
cheesiness
queasiness
uneasiness
wheeziness

REASON
season
treason

REASONABLE
seasonable
treasonable
unreasonable

REASONED
seasoned

REASONING
seasoning

BEAST
ceased
creased
decreased
east
feast
fleeced
greased
increased
leased
least
pieced
policed
priest
released
yeast

EASTER
feaster

B**EASTLY**
priestly

TR**EASURE**
leisure
measure
pleasure
treasure

EASY
breezy
cheesy
queasy
sneezy
uneasy
wheezy

GR**EAT**
see DATE

SW**EAT**
see NET

B**EAT**
beet
bleat
cheat
cleat
compete
complete
conceit
deceit
defeat
delete
discreet
discrete
eat
elite
entreat
feat
feet
fleet
greet
heat
incomplete
mcat
meet
neat
peat
Pete
pleat
receipt
repeat
replete
retreat
seat
sheet
sleet
street
suite
sweet
teat
treat
wheat

SW**EATER**
see BETTER

B**EATER**
cheetah
completer
discreeter
eater
fleeter
heater
litre
meter
metre
neater
Peter
repeater

Rita
sweeter

NEATEST
completest
defeatist
discreetest
fleetest
meetest
neatest
sweetest

BENEATH
heath
Keith
sheath
teeth
underneath
wreath

BREATH
death
saith

BREATHE
bequeath
breathe
seethe
teethe
wreathe

FEATHER
see ALTOGETHER

NEATLY
completely
discreetly
discretely
fleetly
incompletely
neatly
sweetly

NEATNESS
completeness
discreetness
discreteness
incompleteness
neatness
sweetness

CREATURE
see TEACHER

BEAUTIFUL
see DUTIFUL

BEAUTY
see DUTY

LEAVE
see ACHIEVE

HEAVEN
see ELEVEN

BEAVER
believer
deceiver
Eva
fever
Geneva
lever
naiver
receiver
retriever
weaver
(+ leave her *etc*)

B**LEB**
deb
ebb
neb
pleb
web

P**EBBLE**
rebel
treble

D**ECENT**
recent

CH**ECK**
beck
check
cheque
Czech
deck
fleck
heck
peck
reck
speck
trek
wreck

CH**ECKED**
see AFF**ECT**

CH**ECKER**
chequer
pecker
trekker
wrecker

FR**ECKLE**
deckle
freckle
heckle
Jekyll
shekel
speckle

F**ECKLESS**
necklace
reckless
speckless

B**ECKON**
reckon

B**ECKONED**
reckoned
second

CH**ECKS**
becks
checks
cheques
Czechs
decks
ex
flecks
flex
hex
necks
pecks
perplex
Rex
sex
specks
specs
treks
vex
wrecks

AFF**ECT**
bisect

checked
collect
connect
correct
decked
defect (verb)
deflect
detect
direct
dissect
effect
eject
elect
erect
expect
flecked
genuflect
incorrect
indirect
infect
inflect
inject
inspect
intersect
misdirect
necked
neglect
object (verb)
pecked
perfect (verb)
project (verb)
prospect (verb)
protect
recollect
reflect
reject
respect
resurrect
sect
select
specked
subject (verb)
trekked
wrecked

AFF**ECTION**

collection
complexion
confection
connexion
correction
defection
dejection
detection
direction
ejection
election
erection
genuflexion
imperfection
infection
inflection
injection
inspection
intersection
objection
perfection
protection
recollection
reflection
rejection
resurrection
section
selection

COLL**ECTIVE**

corrective
defective
detective
directive
effective

elective
invective
objective
perfective
perspective
prospective
protective
reflective
respective
selective
subjective

COLL**ECTIVELY**
correctively
defectively
effectively
objectively
perfectively
prospectively
protectively
reflectively
respectively
selectively
subjectively

CORR**ECTLY**
directly
erectly
incorrectly
indirectly

COLL**ECTOR**
connector
corrector
defector
deflector
detector
director
ejector
elector
erector
hector
injector
inspector
nectar
objector
projector
prospector
protector
rector
reflector
sector
selector
spectre
vector

DIR**ECTORSHIP**
inspectorship

B**ED**
see AH**EAD**

M**EDAL**
meddle
pedal
peddle
treadle

EDDY
see ALR**EADY**

C**EDE**
see D**EED**

EDGE
allege
dredge
edge
fledge
hedge

kedge
ledge
pledge
Reg
sedge
sledge
wedge

DISOB**EDIENT**
expedient
ingredient
mediant
obedient

AGR**EE**
be
bee
decree
degree
disagree
Dundee
employee
fee
flea
flee
foresee
free
glee
guarantee
he
jubilee
key
knee
lea
lee
me
pea
plea
quay
referee
refugee
scree
sea
see
settee
she
ski
spree
tea
three
tree
trustee

SP**EECH**
see BEACH

D**EED**
agreed
bead
bleed
breed
cede
concede
creed
decreed
deed
disagreed
exceed
feed
freed
greed
guaranteed
heed
impede
indeed
intercede
invalid
kneed
lead (verb)
mead
mislead
need
plead

precede
proceed
read
recede
reed
refereed
seed
skied
speed
stampede
steed
succeed
supersede
Swede
tweed
weed

BL**EEDER**
breeder
leader
pleader
reader

N**EEDLE**
beadle
needle
wheedle

H**EEDLESS**
needless
seedless
weedless

GR**EEDY**
beady
greedy
needy
reedy
seedy
speedy

B**EEF**
see CH**IEF**

CH**EEK**
see B**EAK**

EEL
see APP**EAL**

FR**EELY**
Ely
freely
mealy
steely

S**EEM**
see B**EAM**

S**EEN**
Aberdeen
bean
been
between
clean
convene
dean
demean
demesne
eighteen
fifteen
foreseen
fourteen
gene
glean
green
guillotine
intervene
Jean
keen
lean
machine
magazine

margarine
marine
mean
mien
nineteen
obscene
preen
quarantine
queen
ravine
routine
scene
screen
seen
serene
seventeen
sheen
sixteen
spleen
submarine
thirteen
wean
ween

SCR**EENED**
cleaned
convened
demeaned
fiend
gleaned
guillotined
intervened
preened
quarantined
screened
weaned
weened

GR**EENER**
arena
Argentina
Christina
cleaner
demeanour
Georgina
gleaner
greener
hyena
keener
leaner
meaner
obscener
Selena
serener
subpoena
Tina

GR**EENERY**
deanery
greenery
machinery
plenary
scenery

GR**EENEST**
cleanest
greenest
keenest
leanest
machinist
meanest
obscenest
serenest

GR**EENLY**
cleanly
keenly
meanly
obscenely
routinely
serenely

GR**EENNESS**
cleanness
greenness
keenness
leanness
meanness

ASL**EEP**
cheap
cheep
creep
deep
heap
jeep
keep
leap
neap
oversleep
peep
reap
seep
sheep
sleep
steep
sweep
weep

SL**EEPER**
cheaper
creeper
deeper
keeper
peeper
reaper
sleeper
steeper
sweeper
weeper

ST**EEPLE**
people

D**EEPLY**
cheaply
steeply

B**EER**
see APP**EAR**

AGR**EES**
appease
bees
Belize
breeze
cheese
Chinese
decrees
degrees
disagrees
disease
displease
ease
employees
fees
fleas
flees
foresees
frees
freeze
frieze
glees
guarantees
Japanese
keys
knees
Louise
peas
pleas
please
Portuguese
Pyrenees

quays
referees
refugees
seas
sees
seize
settees
she's
Sinhalese
skis
sneeze
squeeze
Sudanese
teas
tease
telegraphese
these
threes
trapeze
trees
wheeze

GEESE
see **CEASE**

MEET
see **BEAT**

TEETH
see **BENEATH**

SLEEVE
see **ACHIEVE**

FREEZER
appeaser
freezer
geezer
Lisa
Louisa
pleaser
sneezer
squeezer
teaser
Theresa

BREEZY
see **EASY**

CHEF
clef
deaf
Geoff
ref

DEFECT
prefect

PREFER
defer
refer

PREFERENCE
deference
reference

CLEFT
bereft
cleft
deft
eft
heft
left
theft
weft

BEG
dreg
egg
keg
leg

Meg
peg

LEGAL
beagle
eagle
illegal
legal
regal

LEGION
collegian
legion
Norwegian
region

WEIGH
see WAY

NEIGHBOUR
see LABOUR

WEIGHT
see DATE

EIGHTY
Haiti
Katy
maty
slaty
weighty

REIGN
see AGAIN

VEIL
see FRAIL

VEIN
see AGAIN

HEIR
see AFFAIR

LEISURE
see TREASURE

EITHER
blither
either
neither

CONCEIVE
see ACHIEVE

COMPEL
see BELL

HELD
see BELLED

ELDER
welder

ELF
pelf
self
shelf

CELIA
Amelia
Celia
Cordelia
Delia
lobelia
Ophelia

ELK
whelk

BELL
belle

cell
compel
dell
dispel
dwell
excel
expel
farewell
fell
foretell
hell
hotel
impel
knell
lapel
Nell
personnel
propel
quell
rebel (verb)
repel
sell
shell
smell
spell
swell
tell
unwell
well
yell

CELLAR
Della
dweller
feller
propeller
seller
Stella
stellar
teller
yeller
(+ tell a *etc*)

BELLED
beheld
belled
compelled
dispelled
excelled
expelled
felled
geld
held
impelled
knelled
meld
propelled
quelled
rebelled
repelled
shelled
smelled
spelled
swelled
upheld
weld
welled
withheld
yelled

BELLOW
cello
fellow
mellow
yellow

BELLY
Delhi
jelly
Kelly
Nelly

Shelley
smelly

ELM
helm
overwhelm
realm

M**ELON**
Ellen
felon
Helen
Magellan
melon

F**ELONY**
Melanie
miscellany

B**ELT**
Celt
dealt
dwelt
felt
knelt
melt
pelt
smelt
spelt
svelte
veldt
welt

B**ELTER**
felter
kelter
smelter
spelter
swelter
welter

D**ELVE**
helve
shelve
twelve

H**EM**
condemn
gem
hem
phlegm
stem
them

SCH**EMATIC**
thematic

DEC**EMBER**
ember
member
November
remember
September

ASS**EMBLE**
resemble
tremble

EXTR**EME**
see B**EAM**

EXTR**EMELY**
seemly
supremely

ACAD**EMIC**
epidemic
polemic
systemic

ACAD**EMICAL**
chemical
epidemical
polemical

DIL**EMMA**
Emma
lemma
(+ condemn
her *etc*)

ATT**EMPT**
contempt
dreamt
exempt
preempt
tempt
unkempt

AM**EN**
Ben
den
fen
glen
hen
ken
Len
men
pen
ten
then
wen
when
wren
yen

M**ENACE**
Dennis
tennis

LIEUT**ENANT**
pennant
tenant

LIEUT**ENANTS**
penance
pennants
tenants

P**ENCE**
see S**ENSE**

B**ENCH**
blench
clench
drench
French
quench
stench
tench
trench
wench
wrench

TR**ENCHER**
see ADV**ENTURE**

P**ENCIL**
stencil
utensil

B**END**
amend
apprehend
ascend
attend
befriend
bend
blend
commend
comprehend

condescend
contend
defend
depend
descend
distend
end
expend
extend
fend
friend
impend
intend
lend
mend
offend
penned
portend
pretend
recommend
rend
send
spend
suspend
tend
transcend
trend
vend
weekend
wend

ATT**ENDANCE**
ascendance
attendance
defendants
dependence
descendants
independence
pendants
resplendence
superintendents
transcendence

ATT**ENDANT**
ascendant
attendant
defendant
dependent
descendant
independent
pendant
resplendent
superintendent
transcendent

B**ENDER**
agenda
ascender
bender
blender
Brenda
defender
descender
engender
extender
fender
gender
lender
offender
pretender
render
sender
slender
spender
splendour
suspender
surrender
tender
vendor

SL**ENDERER**
tenderer

SLENDEREST
tenderest

SLENDERLY
tenderly

BENDY
effendi
trendy
Wendy

SCENE
see SEEN

LENGTH
strength

LENGTHEN
strengthen

CONVENIENT
inconvenient
lenient

CONVENIENTLY
inconveniently
leniently

BENISON
Tennyson
venison

ANTENNA
duenna
henna
Sienna
tenner
tenor
Vienna
(+ when a *etc*)

TENNIS
see MENACE

PENNY
any
Benny
Jenny
Kenny
Lenny
many
penny

DENS
fens
glens
hens
lens
pens
tens
wens
wrens

SENSE
commence
condense
defence
dense
dispense
expense
fence
hence
immense
intense
offence
pence
pretence
recompense
sense
suspense

tense
thence
whence

DENSELY
immensely
intensely
tensely

PENSION
see ATTENTION

CENSOR
condenser
denser
dispenser
fencer
immenser
intenser
sensor
tenser

DENSEST
immensest
intensest
tensest

SENSIBLE
comprehensible
defensible
indispensable
ostensible
reprehensible
sensible

COMPREH-ENSIVE
apprehensive
defensive
expensive
extensive
inexpensive
offensive
pensive

COMPREH-ENSIVELY
apprehensively
defensively
expensively
extensively
inexpensively
offensively
pensively

BENT
ascent
assent
augment
bent
cement
cent
consent
content
dent
descent
dissent
event
extent
ferment
fragment
frequent (verb)
indent
intent
invent
Kent
lament
leant
lent
meant
pent
present (verb)

prevent
relent
rent
repent
represent
resent
scent
segment (verb)
sent
spent
tent
torment (verb)
vent
went

PREV**ENTABLE**
frequentable
presentable
preventable
rentable

ACCID**ENTAL**
continental
dental
departmental
detrimental
elemental
experimental
fundamental
gentle
governmental
incidental
instrumental
lentil
mental
monumental
occidental
oriental
ornamental
parental
regimental
rental
sacramental
sentimental
temperamental

ARGUM-
ENTATIVE
frequentative
preventative
representative
tentative

ENTER
centre
dissenter
enter
mentor
renter
tenter

CONFID**ENTIAL**
consequential
credential
deferential
differential
essential
existential
influential
pestilential
potential
presidential
prudential
residential
reverential
sequential

APPR**ENTICED**
dentist
intentest

ATT**ENTION**
abstention
apprehension
ascension
attention
comprehension
condescension
convention
declension
detention
dimension
extension
gentian
intention
intervention
invention
mention
ostension
pension
pretension
prevention
retention
suspension
tension

CONV-**ENTIONAL**
intentional

CONV-**ENTIONALLY**
intentionally

ATT**ENTIVE**
incentive
inventive
preventive
retentive

ENTRY
gentry
sentry

ADV**ENTURE**
bencher
denture
misadventure
quencher
trencher
venture

PL**ENTY**
twenty

M**ENU**
venue
(+ then you *etc*)

ING**ENUOUS**
strenuous
tenuous

ING**ENUOUSLY**
strenuously
tenuously

G**ENUS**
venous
Venus

P**EOPLE**
see ST**EEPLE**

Y**EOMAN**
see B**OWMAN**

ST**EP**
cep
hep
pep
prep
rep

skep
step
steppe

LEPER
pepper

SHEPHERD
leopard
peppered
shepherd

INTREPID
tepid

ACCEPT
adept
crept
except
inept
intercept
kept
leapt
pepped
slept
stepped
swept
wept

ANTISEPTIC
epileptic
peptic
sceptic
septic

EXCEPTION
conception
contraception
deception
exception
inception
interception
perception
reception

CONTRAC-
EPTIVE
perceptive

EQUAL
sequel

CHEQUE(R)
see CHECK(ER)

HER
see CUR

ERA
see CLEARER

HERALD
Gerald

HERB
see DISTURB

SHERBET
see BURBOT

PERCH
see CHURCH

MERCY
Circe
mercy
Percy
pursy

HERD(ER)
see ABSURD(ER)

HERE
see APPEAR

WHERE
see AFFAIR

SERF
see TURF

MERGE
see URGE

EMERGENCE
convergence
divergence
emergence
resurgence
submergence

SERIAL
arterial
cereal
ethereal
funereal
imperial
managerial
material
serial

CLERIC
atmospheric
Berwick
cleric
Derek
derrick
Eric
esoteric
exoteric
ferric
generic
Homeric
hysteric
numeric

EXTERIOR
Algeria
blearier
drearier
eerier
exterior
inferior
Liberia
Nigeria
smearier
superior

MYSTERIOUS
deleterious
imperious
mysterious
serious

MYSTERIOUSLY
deleteriously
imperiously
mysteriously
seriously

INHERIT
ferret
inherit
merit

PERJURY
surgery

JERK
see **LURK**

TERM
see **AFFIRM**

DETERMINE
ermine
vermin

HERMIT
permit (noun)
(+ confirm it *etc*)

SERMON
German
Herman
merman
sermon

STERN
see **URN**

INTERNAL
colonel
eternal
external
fraternal
infernal
internal
journal
kernel
maternal
paternal
vernal

STERNEST
earnest
Ernest
sternest

HERO
Nero
zero

FERRET
see **INHERIT**

TERRIFY
verify

ERROR
terror

BERRY
bury
cherry
ferry
Gerry
Kerry
merry
perry
sherry
skerry
Terry
very
wherry

DISPERSAL
rehearsal
reversal
universal

VERSE
adverse
averse
coerce
converse
curse
disperse
diverse

hearse
immerse
inverse
nurse
perverse
purse
rehearse
reimburse
reverse
terse
traverse
verse
worse

IMM**ERSED**
see B**URST**

V**ERSION**
aspersion
assertion
coercion
conversion
desertion
diversion
excursion
exertion
immersion
insertion
inversion
perversion
reversion
submersion
subversion
tertian
version

AL**ERT**
assert
avert
Bert
blurt
convert
curt
desert
dessert
dirt
divert
exert
flirt
girt
hurt
inert
insert
invert
pert
pervert
revert
shirt
skirt
spurt
squirt
wort

C**ERTAIN**
Burton
curtain
uncertain

AL**ERTER**
assertor
converter
curter
deserter
inserter
inverter
perter
perverter

B**ERTH**
see B**IRTH**

SERVE
curve
derv
deserve
nerve
observe
preserve
reserve
serve
swerve
verve

OBSERVABLE
preservable
reservable

FERVENT
observant
servant

PRESENT
see PLEASANT

FLESH
crèche
flesh
fresh
mesh
refresh
thresh

FRESHER
pressure
thresher

PRESIDENT
resident

DESK
burlesque
desk
grotesque
picturesque
statuesque

ADDRESS
assess
Bess
bless
caress
chess
coalesce
compress
confess
cress
depress
digress
distress
dress
duress
effervesce
excess
express
guess
impress
less
mess
ness
nevertheless
obsess
oppress
possess
press
princess
progress
recess
redress
regress
repress
stewardess
stress

success
suppress
transgress
tress
undress
unless
yes

DR**ESSED**
see CH**EST**

V**ESSEL**
see WR**ESTLE**

DR**ESSER**
aggressor
assessor
confessor
dresser
expresser
lesser
oppressor
possessor
professor
successor
suppressor
Tessa

AGGR**ESSION**
compression
confession
depression
digression
discretion
expression
impression
obsession
oppression
possession
procession
progression
recession
regression
repression
secession
session
succession
suppression

AGGR**ESSIVE**
depressive
digressive
excessive
expressive
impressive
obsessive
oppressive
possessive
progressive
recessive
regressive
repressive
suppressive

CH**EST**
abreast
addressed
arrest
assessed
attest
behest
bequest
best
blessed
blest
breast
caressed
chest
compressed
confessed
contest
crest

depressed
detest
digest
digressed
distressed
divest
dressed
effervesced
expressed
guessed
guest
impressed
infest
invest
jest
lest
messed
molest
nest
obsessed
oppressed
pest
possessed
pressed
progressed
protest (verb)
quest
recessed
regressed
repressed
request
rest
stressed
suggest
suppressed
test
transgressed
undressed
unrest
vest
west

F**ESTER**
Chester
fester
investor
jester
Leicester
pester
protester
tester

DIG**ESTION**
congestion
digestion
indigestion
question
suggestion

DIG**ESTIVE**
congestive
digestive
festive
infestive
restive
suggestive

WR**ESTLE**
Cecil
pestle
trestle
vessel
wrestle

N**ET**
abet
ate
beget
bet
brunette
cigarette

debt
duet
epithet
forget
fret
gazette
get
jet
let
met
net
pet
quartet
quintet
regret
rosette
roulette
set
sweat
threat
upset
vet
wet
whet
yet

M**ETAL**

see K**ETTLE**

F**ETCH**

etch
fetch
ketch
retch
sketch
stretch
vetch
wretch

F**ETCHER**

etcher
fletcher
lecher
sketcher
stretcher

COMPL**ETE**

see B**EAT**

M**ETER**

see B**EATER**

ALTOG**ETHER**

feather
heather
leather
nether
tether
together
weather
wether
whether

PATH**ETIC**

aesthetic
alphabetic
anaesthetic
ascetic
athletic
cosmetic
emetic
energetic
genetic
magnetic
pathetic
prophetic
sympathetic
synthetic

B**ETTER**

debtor
letter
setter

sweater
wetter

KETTLE
fettle
metal
mettle
nettle
petal
settle

JETTY
Betty
confetti
jetty
petty
spaghetti
sweaty

EVE
see ACH**IEVE**

ELEVEN
Devon
heaven
leaven
seven

CLEVER
endeavour
ever
forever
however
never
sever
Trevor
whatever
whenever
wherever
whichever
whoever

FEVER
see B**EAVER**

ABBREVIATE
alleviate
deviate

EVIL
medieval
primeval
retrieval
upheaval
weevil

DEVIL
bevel
devil
dishevel
level
Neville
revel

DREW
ado
askew
bamboo
blew
blue
boo
brew
canoe
chew
clue
coo
crew
Crewe
cue
dew
do
drew
due

endue
ensue
eschew
few
flew
flu
flue
glue
gnu
goo
grew
hew
hue
Hugh
imbue
Jew
kangaroo
knew
lasso
loo
mew
moo
new
outdo
overdo
Peru
pew
pursue
queue
renew
review
rue
screw
shampoo
shoe
slew
stew
strew
subdue
sue
taboo
tattoo
threw
through
to
too
true
two
undo
undue
view
who
woo
yew
you
zoo

SHR**EWD**

see N**UDE**

J**EWEL**

see CR**UEL**

F**EWER**

bluer
fewer
newer
pursuer
sewer
truer

F**EWEST**

bluest
canoeist
fewest
newest
shampooist
tattooist
truest

NEWLY
see COOLLY

DEWS
see AMUSE

NEWT
see CUTE

FLEX
see CHECKS

FLEXED
hexed
next
perplexed
sexed
text
vexed

LEXICON
Mexican

COMPLEXION
see AFFECTION

OBEY
see WAY

EYE
see I

I

I

I
apply
awry
aye
belie
buy
by
comply
cry
decry
defy
deny
die
dry
dye
eye
fly
fry
guy
high
I
imply
July
lie
my
nearby
nigh
passerby
pie
ply
pry
rely
reply
rye
shy
sigh
sky
sly
spry
spy
sty
stye
supply
thereby
thigh
thy
tie
try
untie
vie
whereby
why
wry

IABLE

deniable
friable
liable
pliable

reliable
viable

DIAL
see MILE

ALLIANCE
appliance
clients
compliance
defiance
giants
reliance
science

GIANT
client
defiant
giant
reliant

LIAR
see FIRE

DIARY
enquiry
fiery
friary
inquiry
priory
wiry

BIAS
Matthias
pious
Tobias
(+ try us *etc*)

BIB
crib
fib
glib
jib
nib
rib
squib

DRIBBLE
nibble
quibble
scribble

DRIBBLING
nibbling
quibbling
scribbling
sibling

BRIBE
ascribe
bribe
describe
diatribe
gibe
gybe
imbibe
inscribe
jibe
prescribe
proscribe
scribe
subscribe
transcribe
tribe

BRIBER
fibre
giber
imbiber
inscriber
subscriber

Tiber
transcriber

EXHIBIT
inhibit
prohibit

BIBLE
libel
tribal

CONTRIBUTE
attribute
distribute
tribute

TIC
see BRICK

VICAR
see FLICKER

ADVICE
concise
device
dice
entice
ice
lice
mice
nice
precise
price
rice
slice
spice
splice
suffice
thrice
trice
twice
vice

POLICE
see CEASE

DICED
Christ
diced
enticed
iced
priced
sliced
spiced
spliced
sufficed
tryst

NICER
conciser
dicer
enticer
nicer
preciser
slicer

NICEST
concisest
nicest
precisest

RICH
see BITCH

ARTIFICIAL
initial
official
superficial

ARTIFICIALLY
initially

officially
superficially

ICICLE
see B**ICYCLE**

ICIER
dicier
spicier

ICIEST
diciest
spiciest

ICILY
spicily

V**ICIOUS**
see AMB**ITIOUS**

ELECTR**ICITY**
authenticity
complicity
domesticity
duplicity
eccentricity
elasticity
electricity
felicity
multiplicity
publicity
simplicity

BR**ICK**
chick
click
crick
Dick
flick
kick
lick
Mick
nick
pick
prick
quick
rick
sick
slick
snick
stick
thick
tic
tick
trick
wick
wrick

P**ICKED**
see STR**ICT**

QU**ICKEN**
sicken
stricken
thicken

FL**ICKER**
bicker
kicker
knicker
liquor
quicker
sicker
thicker
ticker
tricker
vicar
wicker

QU**ICKEST**
sickest

slickest
thickest

CRICKET
picket
thicket
ticket
wicket
(+ stick it *etc*)

STICKIER
trickier

STICKIEST
trickiest

STICKILY
trickily

STICKINESS
trickiness

FICKLE
nickel
pickle
prickle
sickle
strickle
tickle
trickle

PRICKLY
quickly
sickly
slickly
thickly

SICKNESS
quickness
sickness
slickness
thickness

BRICKS
chicks
cricks
fix
flicks
kicks
licks
mix
nix
picks
pricks
pyx
ricks
six
snicks
sticks
Styx
ticks
transfix
tricks
wicks

STICKY
dicky
Mickey
Nicky
sticky
tricky
Vicky

STRICT
addict (verb)
afflict
bricked
conflict (verb)
contradict
convict (verb)
cricked

depict
derelict
evict
flicked
inflict
kicked
licked
picked
predict
pricked
restrict
ricked
strict
ticked
tricked
wricked

STRICTER
victor

FICTION
addiction
affliction
benediction
contradiction
conviction
crucifixion
depiction
diction
eviction
fiction
friction
infliction
prediction
restriction

PARTICULAR
perpendicular
vehicular

ICY
dicey
spicy

BICYCLE
icicle
tricycle

AMID
bid
chid
did
forbid
grid
hid
id
kid
lid
Madrid
mid
quid
rid
Sid
skid
slid
squid

TIDAL
see BRIDLE

ABIDANCE
guidance
subsidence

HIDDEN
chidden
forbidden
hidden
midden
ridden
stridden

BIDDER
consider
reconsider

MIDDLE
diddle
fiddle
griddle
middle
piddle
riddle
twiddle

ABIDE
applied
aside
beside
bide
bride
chide
coincide
collide
confide
cried
decide
defied
denied
deride
died
divide
dried
dyed
eyed
fried
glide
guide
hide
implied
inside
lied
misguide
outside
override
pied
plied
preside
pride
pried
provide
relied
replied
reside
ride
side
shied
sighed
slide
snide
spied
stride
subside
supplied
tide
tied
tried
untied
vied
wide

CIDER
decider
derider
eider
glider
guider
insider
outsider
provider
rider
slider
spider

strider
wider
(+ beside her *etc*)

CONS**IDER**
see B**IDDER**

ABR**IDGE**
bridge
fridge
midge
ridge

F**IDGET**
Bridget
digit
fidget
midget

BR**IDLE**
bridal
bridle
idle
idol
sidle
suicidal
tidal

K**IDNEY**
Sidney
Sydney

D**IE**
see **I**

CR**IED**
see AB**IDE**

CH**IEF**
beef
belief
brief
chief
fief
grief
leaf
reef
relief
sheaf
thief

BR**IEFLY**
chiefly

BES**IEGE**
liege
siege

F**IELD**
see APP**EALED**

SC**IENCE**
see ALL**IANCE**

FR**IEND**
see B**END**

F**IEND**
see SCR**EENED**

CL**IENT**
see G**IANT**

B**IER**
see APP**EAR**

FL**IER**
see F**IRE**

F**IERCE**
pierce

F**IERIER**
wirier

F**IERIEST**
wiriest

CR**IES**
see ADV**ISE**

DR**IEST**
highest
shiest
slyest
wryest

PR**IEST(LY)**
see B**EAST(LY)**

D**IET**
disquiet
quiet
riot

PROPR**IETOR**
dieter
proprietor
quieter
rioter

ANX**IETY**
impiety
impropriety
notoriety
piety
propriety
sobriety
society
variety

ACH**IEVABLE**
believable
conceivable
perceivable
relievable
retrievable

ACH**IEVE**
aggrieve
believe
bereave
cleave
conceive
deceive
eave
eve
grieve
heave
leave
naive
peeve
perceive
receive
reeve
relieve
reprieve
retrieve
sleeve
Steve
thieve
weave

BEL**IEVER**
see B**EAVER**

IF
see CL**IFF**

LIFE
fife
knife
life
rife
strife
wife

CLIFF
biff
cliff
if
jiff
miff
quiff
skiff
sniff
stiff
tiff
whiff

SNIFFED
see DRIFT

STIFFEN
griffon
gryphon
stiffen

SNIFFER
stiffer

PACIFIC
hieroglyphic
honorific
pacific
prolific
scientific
soporific
specific
terrific

RIFLE
Eiffel
stifle
trifle

DRIFT
biffed
drift
gift
lift
miffed
rift
shift
shrift
sift
sniffed
swift
thrift
whiffed

FIFTY
nifty
shifty
thrifty

BIG
brig
dig
fig
gig
jig
pig
prig
sprig
swig
twig
whig
wig

BIGGER
digger
figure
nigger
rigger
rigour
snigger
trigger
vigour

DIGGING
jigging
rigging
swigging
twigging
wigging

GIGGLE
jiggle
niggle
sniggle
squiggle
wiggle
wriggle
(+ wig'll *etc*)

HIGH
see I

HIGHLAND
island

HIGHLIGHT
skylight
twilight

ALIGHT
bite
blight
bright
cite
contrite
delight
despite
excite
fight
flight
fright
height
ignite
impolite
incite
indict
indite
invite
kite
knight
light
might
mite
night
outright
overnight
plight
polite
quite
recite
recondite
requite
reunite
right
sight
site
slight
smite
spite
sprite
tight
tonight
trite

unite
white
write

BRIGHTEN
Brighton
frighten
heighten
lighten
tighten
Titan
whiten

BRIGHTENING
frightening
heightening
lightening
lightning
tightening
whitening

BRIGHTER
biter
blighter
brighter
fighter
impoliter
inciter
lighter
politer
reciter
slighter
tighter
triter
uniter
whiter
writer

BRIGHTEST
impolitest
lightest
politest
slightest
tightest
tritest
whitest

DELIGHTFUL
frightful
rightful
spiteful

BRIGHTLY
knightly
nightly
politely
rightly
sightly
slightly
spritely
tightly
tritely
unsightly
whitely

BRIGHTNESS
impoliteness
lightness
politeness
rightness
slightness
tightness
triteness
whiteness

ALMIGHTY
Aphrodite
blighty
flighty
mighty

RIGID
Brigid
frigid
rigid

RELIGION
pigeon
religion
smidgeon
widgeon

PRODIGIOUS
religious
sacrilegious

DIGIT
see FIDGET

SIGN
see BRINE

DESIGNER
see FINER

DIGNIFY
lignify
signify

BIGOT
frigate
spigot

VIGOUR
see BIGGER

FATIGUE
intrigue
league

FIGURE
see BIGGER

ALIKE
bike
dislike
dyke
hike
like
Mike
pike
shrike
spike
strike
tyke
unlike

HIKER
mica
pica
striker

NIL
see BILL

FILBERT
Gilbert

GILD
see CHILLED

CHILD
beguiled
child
compiled
defiled
dialled
filed
mild
piled
reviled
riled
smiled
styled

tiled
wild
wiled

MILDER
wilder

BEWILDER
builder
gilder
guilder
Hilda

MILDEST
wildest

MILDLY
wildly

MILE
aisle
beguile
bile
Carlisle
compile
defile
denial
dial
file
guile
I'll
isle
mile
Nile
phial
pile
revile
rile
smile
stile
style
tile
trial
vile
viol
while
wile
worthwhile

FILED
see CHILD

MILER
compiler
defiler
reviler
smiler
tiler
viler

SKILFUL
wilful

SKILFULLY
wilfully

ABILITY
acceptability
agility
availability
civility
credibility
debility
desirability
disability
docility
facility
feasibility
fertility
flexibility
fragility

futility
hostility
humility
impossibility
inability
inevitability
infallibility
inflexibility
liability
nobility
possibility
probability
responsibility
sensibility
servility
sterility
tranquillity
utility
versatility
virility
visibility

MILK
bilk
ilk
milk
silk

BILL
Brazil
chill
daffodil
distil
downhill
drill
fill
frill
fulfil
gill
grill
hill
ill
instil
Jill
kill
mill
nil
Phil
pill
quill
rill
shrill
sill
skill
spill
still
swill
thrill
till
trill
twill
until
uphill
will

PILLAGE
tillage
village

CHILLED
billed
build
chilled
distilled
drilled
filled
frilled
fulfilled
gild
grilled
guild
instilled

killed
milled
skilled
spilled
thrilled
tilled
trilled
twilled
willed

C**HILLER**
caterpillar
chiller
distiller
filler
gorilla
guerrilla
killer
miller
pillar
shriller
stiller
thriller

C**HILLEST**
illest
shrillest
stillest

B**ILLET**
fillet
millet
skillet
(+ kill it *etc*)

C**HILLIER**
frillier
hillier
sillier

C**HILLIEST**
frilliest
hilliest
silliest

B**ILLION**
Brazilian
million
pavilion
pillion
postillion
trillion
vermilion

C**HILLNESS**
illness
shrillness
stillness

P**ILLOW**
armadillo
billow
pillow
willow

C**HILLY**
Chile
filly
frilly
hilly
lily
Millie
shrilly
silly
willy-nilly

H**ILT**
built
gilt
guilt
hilt

jilt
kilt
lilt
quilt
silt
spilt
stilt
tilt
wilt

FILTH
tilth

WILY
dryly
highly
shyly
slyly
wily
wryly

BRIM
dim
grim
him
hymn
Jim
Kim
limb
limn
prim
rim
skim
slim
swim
Tim
trim
vim
whim

LIMBER
timber

NIMBLE
cymbal
gimbal
nimble
symbol
thimble

CHIME
climb
crime
dime
grime
halftime
I'm
lime
mime
prime
rhyme
slime
sublime
thyme
time

TIMER
climber
primer
rhymer
timer

DIMLY
grimly
primly
slimly
trimly

DIMMER
glimmer
grimmer

primmer
simmer
slimmer
swimmer
trimmer

DIMMEST
grimmest
primmest
slimmest
trimmest

GIMMICK
mimic

IMP
blimp
chimp
crimp
imp
limp
pimp
scrimp
shrimp
skimp

LIMPER
simper
whimper

DIMPLE
pimple
simple
wimple

DIMPLY
limply
pimply
simply

GLIMPSE
blimps
chimps
crimps
imps
limps
pimps
scrimps
shrimps
skimps

BEGIN
akin
begin
bin
chin
din
fin
Finn
gin
grin
in
inn
kin
paraffin
pin
shin
sin
skin
spin
thin
tin
twin
violin
win
within

FINAL
spinal

CONV**INCE**
chintz
convince
evince
flints
glints
hints
mince
mints
prince
prints
quince
rinse
since
splints
sprints
squints
stints
tints
wince

INCH
cinch
clinch
finch
flinch
inch
lynch
pinch
winch

DIST**INCT**
see BL**INKED**

BEH**IND**
assigned
behind
bind
blind
combined
confined
consigned
declined
defined
designed
dined
divined
enshrined
find
fined
grind
hind
inclined
kind
lined
maligned
mankind
mind
pined
refined
remind
resigned
rind
signed
twined
underlined
undermined
whined
wind
wined

W**IND**
see GR**INNED**

C**INDER**
hinder
Linda
tinder

B**INDER**
blinder

finder
grinder
kinder
minder
reminder
winder

BL**INDEST**
kindest

W**INDIER**
India

DW**INDLE**
kindle
spindle
swindle

BL**INDLY**
kindly
resignedly

BR**INE**
assign
benign
brine
chine
combine
confine
consign
decline
define
design
dine
divine
enshrine
entwine
fine
incline
kine
line
malign
mine
nine
pine
recline
refine
repine
resign
shine
shrine
sign
spine
swine
syne
thine
twine
underline
undermine
vine
whine
wine

MAR**INE**
see S**EEN**

L**INED**
see BEH**IND**

DIV**INELY**
benignly
divinely
finely
malignly

F**INER**
benigner
china
definer
designer
diner

diviner
finer
liner
maligner
miner
minor
refiner
shiner
signer

DIVINEST
benignest
finest
malignest

BRING
cling
fling
king
ling
ping
ring
sing
sling
spring
sting
string
swing
thing
wing
wring

FRINGE
binge
cringe
fringe
hinge
impinge
singe
swinge
syringe
tinge
twinge

GINGER
injure

BRINGER
humdinger
ringer
singer
slinger
stringer
swinger
winger
wringer
(+ sing a *etc*)

FINGER
linger
malinger

JINGLE
ingle
jingle
mingle
shingle
single
surcingle
tingle

CLINIC
cynic

SHINIER
brinier
shinier
spinier
tinier
winier

SHINIEST
briniest
shiniest
spiniest
tiniest
winiest

DOMINION
minion
opinion
pinion

DIMINISH
finish
Finnish
thinnish

ADMINISTER
minister
sinister

AFFINITY
divinity
femininity
infinity
masculinity
trinity
vicinity
virginity

BLINK
brink
chink
clink
drink
ink
jink
kink
link
mink
pink
rink
shrink
sink
slink
stink
think
wink
zinc

BLINKED
chinked
clinked
distinct
extinct
inked
instinct
jinked
linked
pinked
precinct
succinct
tinct
winked

BLINKER
clinker
drinker
pinker
shrinker
sinker
stinker
thinker
tinker
winker

CRINKLE
sprinkle
tinkle
twinkle

winkle
wrinkle

BL**INKS**
brinks
chinks
clinks
drinks
inks
jinks
jinx
kinks
links
lynx
methinks
minks
minx
pinks
rinks
shrinks
sinks
slinks
sphinx
stinks
thinks
winks

GR**INNED**
pinned
shinned
sinned
skinned
thinned
tinned
twinned
wind

D**INNER**
beginner
dinner
inner
sinner
skinner
thinner
winner

TH**INNEST**
violinist

L**INNET**
minute
spinet
(+ begin it *etc*)

N**INNY**
finny
Ginny
guinea
hinny
mini
Minnie
ninny
Pliny
skinny
spinney
tinny
whinny

R**INSE**
see CONV**INCE**

M**INSTER**
spinster
(+ convinced her *etc*)

H**INT**
dint
flint
glint
hint

lint
mint
print
skint
splint
sprint
squint
stint
tint

MINTER
printer
splinter
sprinter
squinter
winter

MINX
see BLINKS

SHINY
briny
shiny
spiny
tiny
winy

LION
Brian
ion
iron
lion
scion
(+ eye on *etc*)

RIOT
see DIET

PIOUS
see BIAS

CHIP
clip
dip
drip
equip
flip
grip
hip
kip
lip
nip
pip
rip
scrip
ship
sip
skip
slip
snip
strip
tip
trip
whip
zip

PIPE
gripe
hype
pipe
ripe
snipe
stripe
swipe
tripe
type
wipe

PIPER
riper
sniper

viper
wiper

RIPEST
typist

EQUIPMENT
shipment

CHIPPED
clipped
crypt
dipped
dripped
equipped
gripped
nipped
pipped
ripped
script
shipped
sipped
skipped
slipped
stripped
tipped
tripped
whipped
zipped

CLIPPER
dipper
flipper
gripper
kipper
nipper
Pippa
ripper
shipper
skipper
slipper
stripper
tipper
tripper
whipper
zipper

CRIPPLE
fipple
nipple
ripple
stipple
tipple
triple

CRIPPLING
rippling
stippling
stripling
tippling
tripling

CHIPS
clips
dips
drips
eclipse
ellipse
equips
flips
grips
hips
kips
lips
nips
pips
rips
ships
sips
skips
slips
snips

strips
tips
trips
whips
zips

SCRIPT
see CHIPPED

DESCRIPTION
ascription
conscription
description
Egyptian
inscription
prescription
proscription
subscription

MANIPULATE
stipulate

UNIQUE
see BEAK

LIQUOR
see FLICKER

FIR
see CUR

DESIRABLE
acquirable
desirable
expirable
requirable
untirable

BIRCH
see CHURCH

GIRD(ER)
see ABSURD(ER)

GIRDLE
see CURDLE

FIRE
acquire
admire
aspire
attire
briar
brier
buyer
choir
conspire
desire
dire
drier
dyer
enquire
entire
esquire
expire
fire
flier
friar
gyre
higher
hire
inquire
inspire
ire
liar
lyre
mire
misfire
nigher
perspire
prior
quire

require
retire
shier
shire
sire
slier
spire
squire
supplier
tire
transpire
tyre
wire
wryer

IRK
see **LURK**

G**IRL**
see C**URL**

AFF**IRM**
confirm
firm
germ
infirm
perm
sperm
squirm
term
therm
worm

F**IRMER**
Burma
firmer
infirmer
murmur
squirmer
wormer

CH**IRP**
see B**URP**

CH**IRRUP**
stirrup
syrup

F**IRST**
see B**URST**

D**IRT**
see AL**ERT**

B**IRTH**
berth
birth
dearth
earth
firth
girth
mirth
Perth
worth

D**IRTY**
Bertie
flirty
Gertie
shirty
thirty

H**IS**
is
fizz
Liz
quiz
whiz

CONC**ISE**
see ADV**ICE**

ADVISE
allies
applies
arise
belies
buys
complies
comprise
cries
decries
defies
denies
despise
devise
dies
disguise
dries
dyes
eyes
flies
fries
guise
guys
implies
lies
nighs
pies
plics
pries
prize
relies
replies
revise
rise
shies
sighs
size
skies
spies
sties
styes
supplies
surmise
surprise
thighs
ties
tries
unties
vies
wise

CHISEL
see FIZZLE

ADVISER
deviser
miser
reviser
riser
wiser

DISH
fish
swish
wish

COLLISION
decision
derision
division
precision
prevision
provision
revision
vision

BRISK
disc
frisk
risk
whisk

BR**ISKER**
whisker

FR**ISKY**
pisky
risky
whisky

ISLAND
see H**IGHLAND**

CHR**ISM**
prism
schism

PR**ISON**
arisen
mizzen
prison
risen
wizen

CR**ISP**
lisp
wisp

CR**ISPER**
lisper
whisper

M**ISS**
abyss
amiss
bliss
Chris
dismiss
hiss
kiss
miss
remiss
Swiss
this

M**ISSAL**
see BR**ISTLE**

M**ISSED**
see ASS**IST**

M**ISSES**
abysses
blisses
dismisses
hisses
kisses
misses
mrs
(+ this is *etc*)

M**ISSION**
see ADD**ITION**

ISSUE
tissue
(+ miss you *etc*)

ASS**IST**
consist
cyst
dismissed
exist
fist
grist
hissed
insist
journalist
kissed
list
missed
mist

persist
resist
tryst
twist
whist
wrist

CHR**IST**
see D**ICED**

ASS**ISTANCE**
consistence
distance
existence
inconsistence
insistence
persistence
resistance

ASS**ISTANT**
consistent
distant
inconsistent
insistent
persistent
resistant

CHR**ISTEN**
glisten
listen
Nissen

CONS-
ISTENTLY
distantly
inconsistently
insistently
persistently

BL**ISTER**
glister
mister
sister
reșister
transistor
twister
vista
(+ kissed her *etc*)

PR**ISTINE**
Christine
pristine
Sistine

BR**ISTLE**
dismissal
epistle
gristle
missal
thistle
whistle
(+ this'll *etc*)

P**ISTOL**
Bristol
crystal
pistol

H**ISTORY**
blistery
history
mystery

ACQU**IT**
admit
bit
chit
commit
emit
fit
flit

grit
hit
it
kit
knit
lit
mitt
omit
permit
pit
quit
remit
sit
skit
slit
spit
split
submit
tit
transmit
twit
wit
writ

RE**CITAL**
entitle
recital
requital
title
vital

B**ITCH**
ditch
flitch
hitch
itch
niche
pitch
quitch
rich
stitch
switch
twitch
which
witch

P**ITCHER**
richer
twitcher

B**ITE**
see AL**IGHT**

EXC**ITEMENT**
incitement
indictment

P**ITH**
fifth
kith
myth
pith
smith
with

BL**ITHE**
lithe
scythe
tithe
writhe

D**ITHER**
hither
slither
whither
wither
zither

INITIAL(LY)
see
ARTIFICIAL(LY)

CRITIC
analytic
critic
paralytic
parasitic

CRITICAL
analytical
hypocritical
political

ADDITION
abolition
acquisition
addition
admission
admonition
ambition
ammunition
apparition
audition
coalition
commission
competition
composition
condition
definition
disposition
edition
electrician
exhibition
expedition
exposition
fission
fruition
ignition
imposition
inhibition
intuition
magician
mission
musician
nutrition
omission
opposition
optician
partition
permission
petition
physician
politician
position
preposition
prohibition
proposition
recognition
repetition
sedition
statistician
submission
superstition
supposition
suspicion
tactician
tradition
transition
transmission

ADDITIONAL
compositional
conditional
nutritional
positional
prepositional
traditional
transitional
unconditional

AMB**ITIOUS**
auspicious
avaricious
capricious
delicious
factitious
fictitious
judicious
malicious
meretricious
officious
pernicious
propitious
repetitious
seditious
superstitious
suppositious
suspicious
vicious

T**ITLE**
see REC**ITAL**

ACQU**ITS**
admits
bits
blitz
commits
grits
its
it's
kits
knits
omits
permits
pits
quits
sits
slits
splits
spits
submits
transmits
wits

WR**ITTEN**
Britain
Briton
kitten
mitten
smitten
written

B**ITTER**
fitter
flitter
fritter
glitter
hitter
jitter
knitter
litter
quitter
sitter
splitter
titter
transmitter
twitter

B**ITTERLY**
Italy

BR**ITTLE**
little
noncommittal
skittle
spittle
tittle
victual
whittle

CITY
bitty
city
committee
ditty
gritty
kitty
pity
pretty
witty

ARRIVAL
revival
rival
survival

ALIVE
arrive
chive
Clive
connive
contrive
deprive
derive
dive
drive
five
hive
jive
live
revive
shrive
skive
strive
survive
thrive
wive

FORGIVE
give
live
misgive
sieve

SWIVEL
civil
drivel
shrivel
snivel
swivel

DELIVER
giver
liver
quiver
river
shiver
sliver

DIVER
driver
fiver

ARRIVES
chives
connives
contrives
deprives
derives
dives
drives
fives
hives
jives
knives
lives
revives
shrives
skives
strives
survives

thrives
wives

TRIVIA
Bolivia
Livia
Olivia
Olivier
trivia

LIVID
vivid

LIVIDLY
vividly

FIX
see BRICKS

CRUCIFIXION
see FICTION

FIXTURE
mixture

BLIZZARD
gizzard
lizard
scissored
vizard
wizard

SIZE
see ADVISE

DIZZIER
busier
dizzier
frizzier
Tunisia

DIZZIEST
busiest
dizziest
frizziest

FIZZLE
chisel
drizzle
frizzle
grizzle
mizzle
pizzle
sizzle
swizzle
twizzle

DIZZY
busy
dizzy
frizzy
Lizzy
tizzy
(+ is he *etc*)

O

AGO
see BLOW

DO
see DREW

APPROACH
broach
brooch
coach
encroach
loach
poach
reproach
roach

ROAD
see ABODE

LOAF
oaf

OAK
see AWOKE

COAL
see HOLE

FOAM
see COMB

GROAN
see ALONE

SOAP
see COPE

BOAR
see ADORE

BOARD
see CORD

COARSE
see HORSE

COARSELY
hoarsely

COARSER
Chaucer
coarser
courser
endorser
hoarser
reinforcer
saucer

COARSEST
hoarsest

BOAST
see POST

BOASTER
coaster
poster
roaster
toaster

GOAT
see NOTE

BOATER
see VOTER

OATH
see BOTH

LOATHE
see CLOTHE

HOAX
blokes
chokes
cloaks
coax
croaks
evokes
folks
hoax
invokes
jokes
oaks
pokes
provokes
revokes
smokes
soaks
stokes
strokes
yokes
yolks

BLOB
bob
cob
fob
gob
hob
job
knob
lob
mob
nob
rob
slob
snob
sob
squab
swab
throb

CLOBBER
cobber
jobber
robber
slobber

BOBBLE
cobble
gobble
hobble
knobble
nobble
squabble
wobble

WOBBLY
cobbly
knobbly

squabbly
wobbly

HOBBY
bobby
hobby
knobby
lobby
snobby

GLOBE
Job
lobe
probe
robe

OCTOBER
prober
sober

LOBSTER
mobster

LOCAL
focal
local
vocal
yokel

LOCALLY
focally
locally
vocally

OCEAN
see EMOTION

BLOCK
chock
clock
cock
crock
dock
flock
frock
hock
Jock
knock
loch
lock
mock
o'clock
pock
rock
shock
smock
sock
stock
unlock

BLOCKED
clocked
cocked
concoct
decoct
docked
flocked
knocked
locked
mocked
rocked
shocked
socked
stocked
unlocked

BLOCKER
cocker
docker
knocker

locker
mocker
ocker
rocker
shocker
soccer
stocker

CR**OCKERY**
mockery
rockery

P**OCKET**
docket
locket
pocket
rocket
socket
sprocket
(+ mock it *etc*)

BL**OCKS**
box
chocks
clocks
cocks
cox
crocks
docks
flocks
fox
hocks
knocks
locks
mocks
ox
pox
rocks
shocks
smocks
socks
stocks
unlocks

C**OCKY**
hockey
jockey
oche
pocky
rocky
stocky

ARIST**OCRACY**
bureaucracy
democracy

MEDI**OCRE**
see BR**OKER**

CONC**OCT**
see BL**OCKED**

D**OCTOR**
concocter
decocter
doctor
proctor
(+ socked her *etc*)

CR**OCUS**
focus
locus
hocus-pocus
(+ woke us *etc*)

FOC**USSED**
locust

C**OD**
bod
clod
cod

god
hod
mod
nod
odd
plod
pod
prod
quad
rod
shod
sod
squad
trod
wad

S**ODA**
coda
exploder
loader
odour
pagoda
soda
unloader

TR**ODDEN**
modern
sodden
trodden

G**ODDESS**
bodice

C**ODDLE**
doddle
model
noddle
toddle
twaddle
waddle

C**ODDLER**
modeller
toddler

SH**ODDY**
see B**ODY**

AB**ODE**
bestowed
bode
code
corrode
crowed
erode
explode
flowed
forebode
glowed
goad
hoed
load
lode
mode
mowed
node
ode
overflowed
owed
road
rode
sewed
showed
slowed
snowed
sowed
stowed
strode
toad
towed

unload
woad

MODEST
oddest

DODGE
bodge
dodge
lodge
podge
stodge

LODGER
bodger
dodger
lodger
Roger

METHODICAL
periodical
rhapsodical
spasmodical

ODOUR
see SODA

BODY
shoddy
swaddy
wadi

FOE
see BLOW

FOES
see AROSE

SHOES
see AMUSE

DOES
see BUZZ

OFF
cough
doff
off
quaff
scoff
toff
trough

COFFEE
toffee

OFFER
coffer
offer
quaffer
scoffer

ALOFT
coughed
croft
doffed
loft
oft
quaffed
scoffed
soft
waft

OFTEN
soften

SOFTER
crofter
(+ waft her *etc*)

BOG
clog
cog
dog
flog
fog
frog
grog
hog
jog
log
slog

YOGA
ogre
toga
yoga

FLOGGER
jogger
slogger

BOGGLE
goggle
joggle
toggle
(+ dog'll *etc*)

FOGGY
boggy
doggy
foggy
Froggy
groggy
soggy

AUTOBI-OGRAPHY
bibliography
biography
cosmography
cryptography
geography
hagiography
lexicography
photography
physiography
pornography
topography
typography

BROGUE
prorogue
rogue
vogue

HEROIC
stoic

CHOICE
Joyce
rejoice
voice

VOICED
see HOIST

AVOID
see TOYED

BOIL
broil
coil
despoil
foil
loyal
oil
recoil
royal
soil
spoil
toil

BOILER
broiler
oiler
soiler
spoiler
toiler

COIN
groin
join
loin
purloin
quoin

APPOINT
anoint
appoint
disappoint
joint
point

APPOINTMENT
disappointment
ointment

NOISE
see ANNOYS

HOIST
foist
hoist
moist
rejoiced
voiced

CLOISTER
moister
oyster
roister

ADROIT
Detroit
exploit
quoit

ADROITER
goitre
loiter
reconnoitre

AWOKE
bloke
broke
choke
cloak
coke
croak
evoke
folk
invoke
joke
oak
poke
provoke
revoke
smoke
soak
spoke
stoke
stroke
woke
yoke
yolk

YOKEL
see LOCAL

BROKEN
oaken
outspoken
spoken

token
woken

BROKENLY
outspokenly

BROKER
choker
joker
mediocre
ochre
pawnbroker
poker
smoker
stoker
stroker

CHOKES
see HOAX

SOLAR
see CONTROLLER

BOLD
bowled
cajoled
cold
condoled
consoled
controlled
doled
extolled
fold
gold
hold
mould
old
patrolled
polled
rolled
scold
sold
strolled
told
tolled
unfold
uphold
withhold
wold

BEHOLDEN
embolden
golden
olden
(+ cold 'un *etc*)

BOLDER
beholder
bolder
boulder
colder
folder
holder
moulder
older
shoulder
smoulder
upholder
(+ scold her *etc*)

BOLDEST
coldest
oldest

BOLDLY
coldly

HOLE
bole

bowl
cajole
coal
condole
console
control
dole
droll
extol
foal
goal
hole
mole
parole
patrol
pole
poll
role
roll
scroll
shoal
sole
stole
stroll
toll
vole
whole

ST**OLEN**
swollen

LIN**OLEUM**
petroleum
scholium

FR**OLIC**
alcoholic
bucolic
colic
diabolic
frolic
melancholic
rollick
symbolic

S**OLID**
jollied
solid
squalid
stolid
volleyed

H**OLIER**
lowlier
magnolia
Mongolia

H**OLIEST**
lowliest

AB**OLISH**
demolish
polish

F**OLK**
see AW**OKE**

R**OLL**
see H**OLE**

D**OLL**
atoll
doll
loll
moll

C**OLLAR**
choler
collar
dollar
holler

scholar
squalor

COLLEGE
see
ACKN**OWLEDGE**

CONTR**OLLER**
bowler
droller
extoller
molar
patroller
polar
roller
solar
stroller

V**OLLEYED**
see S**OLID**

M**OLLIFY**
disqualify
jollify
mollify
qualify

C**OLLOP**
dollop
lollop
scallop
trollop
Trollope
wallop

F**OLLOW**
Apollo
follow
hollow
swallow
wallow

F**OLLOWER**
hollower
swallower
wallower

D**OLLY**
folly
golly
holly
jolly
melancholy
Molly
Polly
trolley
volley
Wally

P**OLO**
solo
(+ grow low *etc*)

ANTH**OLOGY**
anthropology
apology
archaeology
astrology
biology
chronology
geology
hagiology
meteorology
mythology
pathology
philology
phraseology
psychology
sociology
technology

terminology
theology
zoology

C**OLONEL**
see INT**ERNAL**

C**OLOUR**
see D**ULLER**

B**OLSTER**
holster
upholster

B**OLT**
colt
dolt
holt
jolt
moult
revolt
smolt
volt

C**OLUMN**
solemn

ABS**OLVE**
devolve
dissolve
evolve
involve
resolve
revolve
solve

H**OLY**
see SL**OWLY**

FR**OM**
aplomb
bomb
from
prom
rhomb
Tom

R**OMAN**
see B**OWMAN**

C**OMB**
chrome
comb
dome
foam
gnome
home
loam
ohm
roam
Rome
tome

T**OMB**
see ASS**UME**

C**OMBAT**
wombat

C**OMBER**
Cromer
homer
roamer

C**OME**
see DR**UM**

D**OME**
see C**OMB**

OMEN
see **BOWMAN**

C**OMET**
grommet
vomit
(+ from it *etc*)

KIL**OMETER**
speedometer
thermometer

AT**OMIC**
astronomic
comic
economic
gastronomic
taxonomic

D**OMINATE**
abominate
dominate
nominate

P**OMP**
romp
swamp

PR**OMPT**
romped
swamped

ON
anon
Bonn
con
don
gone
John
on
Ron
shone
swan
upon
whereupon
Yvonne

S**ON**
see B**UN**

ENSC**ONCE**
nonce
response
sconce

ONCE
see D**UNCE**

BEY**OND**
abscond
beyond
blond(e)
bond
conned
correspond
donned
fond
frond
pond
respond
second (verb)
wand

M**ONDAY**
Sunday

ABSC**ONDER**
blonder
fonder
ponder
responder
seconder

squander
wander
yonder

WONDER
see **BLUNDER**

BLONDEST
fondest

ALONE
atone
blown
bone
Cologne
cone
crone
dethrone
drone
flown
groan
grown
hone
Joan
known
loan
lone
moan
mown
own
phone
postpone
prone
roan
sewn
shown
sown
stone
throne
thrown
tone
unknown
zone

GONE
see **ON**

DONE
see **BUN**

LONELY
only

LONER
Barcelona
donor
groaner
loner
moaner
owner

GONER
honour
(+ on her *etc*)

HONEST
wannest

HONEY
see **FUNNY**

ALONG
belong
bong
gong
long
pong
prolong
prong
song

strong
thong
throng
tong
wrong

AM**ONG**
see **BUNG**

SP**ONGE**
see PL**UNGE**

L**ONGER**
conga
conger
longer
stronger
Tonga

L**ONGEST**
strongest

STR**ONGLY**
wrongly

T**ONGUE**
see **BUNG**

CHR**ONIC**
conic
electronic
harmonic
ironic
laconic
sardonic
supersonic
symphonic
tonic

ONION
see B**UNION**

ADM**ONISH**
astonish

M**ONK**
see B**UNK**

ONLY
see L**ONELY**

D**ONNED**
see BEY**OND**

B**ONNET**
sonnet
(+ on it *etc*)

ASTR**ONOMY**
gastronomy
economy
taxonomy

C**ONSUL**
tonsil

FR**ONT**
see BL**UNT**

DON'T
won't
wont

B**ONUS**
onus
(+ phone us *etc*)

B**ONY**
crony
macaroni

phoney
pony
stony
Tony

B**OO**
see DR**EW**

BR**OOCH**
see APPR**OACH**

G**OOD**
could
good
hood
should
stood
understood
withstood
wood
would

F**OOD**
see N**UDE**

BL**OOD**
see M**UD**

D**OODLE**
caboodle
canoodle
doodle
feudal
noodle
poodle

H**OOF**
aloof
behoof
goof
hoof
proof
reproof
roof
spoof
woof

ST**OOGE**
see H**UGE**

B**OOK**
brook
cook
crook
forsook
hook
look
mistook
nook
overlook
overtook
partook
rook
shook
stook
took
undertook

SP**OOK**
see D**UKE**

B**OOKER**
cooker
hooker
looker

C**OOL**
drool
fool
pool
rule
school

spool
stool
tool
you'll
yule

WOOL
see BULL

COOLER
ruler

COOLISH
foolish

COOLLY
duly
newly
truly

ROOM
see ASSUME

AFTERNOON
baboon
balloon
bassoon
boon
buffoon
cartoon
cocoon
croon
dragoon
dune
goon
harpoon
hewn
immune
impugn
June
lagoon
lampoon
loon
maroon
monsoon
moon
noon
oppugn
platoon
pontoon
prune
saloon
soon
spoon
strewn
swoon
tune
tycoon
typhoon

CROONER
harpooner
impugner
lampooner
oppugner
pruner
sooner
tuner

BALLOONIST
cartoonist
immunest
lampoonist
soonest

LOONY
moony
puny
Rooney
spoony

COOP
croup
droop
dupe
group
hoop
loop
poop
scoop
sloop
soup
stoop
stoup
swoop
troop
troupe
whoop

COOPER
grouper
Hooper
looper
scooper
super
swooper
trooper

DOOR(S)
see ADORE(s)

POOR
see ADORE, CURE

DOORMAN
foreman
Norman

DOORWAY
Norway

GOOSE
see PRODUCE

LOOSED, BOOST
see PRODUCED

FOOT
put
soot

BOOT
see CUTE

TOOTH
booth
forsooth
Ruth
sleuth
tooth
truth
uncouth
youth

SMOOTH
soothe

OOZE
see AMUSE

CHOP
cop
crop
drop
flop
fop
hop
lop
mop
nonstop
op

plop
pop
prop
shop
slop
sop
stop
strop
swap
top
whop

COPE
dope
elope
grope
hope
lope
mope
Pope
rope
scope
slope
soap
trope

PROPER
see CHOPPER

IMPROPERLY
monopoly
properly

TROPHY
Sophie
strophe
trophy

TOPIC
kaleidoscopic
microscopic
misanthropic
myopic
philanthropic
telescopic
topic
tropic

TOPICAL
kaleidoscopical
microscopical
philanthropical
topical
tropical

CROPPED
adopt
chopped
copped
cropped
dropped
flopped
hopped
lopped
mopped
opt
plopped
popped
propped
shopped
slopped
stopped
stropped
swapped
topped
whopped

CHOPPER
copper

dropper
hopper
improper
popper
proper
shopper
stopper
topper
whopper

CH**OPPY**
copy
floppy
poppy
sloppy
soppy

OPT
see CR**OPPED**

OR
see AD**ORE**

C**ORAL**
choral
coral
floral
immoral
laurel
moral
oral
quarrel
sorrel

ABS**ORB**
adsorb
orb
resorb

F**ORCE**
see H**ORSE**

P**ORCH**
debauch
porch
scorch
torch

SC**ORCHER**
see T**ORTURE**

C**ORD**
abhorred
aboard
abroad
accord
adored
afford
applaud
award
awed
board
bored
broad
chord
Claud
clawed
cord
cored
defraud
deplored
explored
floored
ford
fraud
gnawed
gored
hoard
horde
ignored
implored

jawed
lord
Maud
pawed
pored
poured
record (verb)
restored
reward
roared
scored
shored
snored
soared
stored
sward
sword
thawed
ward
warred
whored

W**ORD**
see ABS**URD**

ACC**ORDED**
afforded
applauded
awarded
boarded
corded
defrauded
forded
hoarded
lorded
recorded
rewarded
sordid
warded
(+ four did *etc*)

B**ORDER**
applauder
boarder
border
broader
disorder
hoarder
order
recorder
warder

ACC**ORDING**
affording
applauding
awarding
boarding
cording
fording
hoarding
lording
recording
rewarding

C**ORDON**
Gordon
Jordan
warden
(+ poured an *etc*)

AD**ORE**
abhor
adore
ashore
assure
awe
before
boar
bore
braw

chore
claw
core
corps
deplore
door
draw
drawer
explore
flaw
floor
for
fore
four
furthermore
gnaw
gore
haw
hoar
ignore
implore
insure
jaw
law
lore
maw
moor
more
nor
oar
or
ore
outdoor
paw
poor
pore
pour
raw
reassure
restore
roar
saw
score
shore
Singapore
snore
soar
sore
spore
store
straw
sure
swore
taw
thaw
tore
war
whore
withdraw
wore
yore
(Some of these words have an alternative pronunciation rhyming with CURE.)

BORED

see CORD

FOREHEAD

see HORRID

SORELY

poorly
rawly
sorely
surely

AD*ORER*
abhorrer
aura
borer
deplorer
Dora
explorer
flora
ignorer
implorer
Laura
Nora
poorer
pourer
restorer
roarer
scorer
snorer
soarer
sorer
storer
(+ wore a *etc*)

AD*ORES*
abhors
adores
applause
awes
boars
bores
cause
chores
clause
claws
cores
deplores
doors
draws
drawers
explores
flaws
floors
gauze
gnaws
gores
hawse
ignores
implores
indoors
jaws
laws
oars
ores
outdoors
pause
paws
pores
pours
restores
roars
saws
scores
shores
snores
soars
sores
spores
stores
straws
taws
tawse
thaws
wars
whores
withdraws
yours

S*OREST*
hoarest
poorest
sorest

FORGE
disgorge
forge
George
gorge

GLORIOUS
censorious
glorious
inglorious
laborious
meritorious
notorious
uproarious
uxorious
victorious

AUTHORITY
inferiority
majority
minority
priority
superiority

FORK
baulk
chalk
cork
fork
gawk
hawk
pork
stalk
stork
talk
torque
walk
York

WORK
see LURK

WORLD
see CURLED

FORM
conform
corm
deform
dorm
form
inform
lukewarm
norm
perform
reform
storm
swarm
transform
warm

WORM
see AFFIRM

FORMAL
informal
normal

FORMER
dormer
former
informer
lukewarmer
Norma
performer
reformer
transformer
warmer

ADORN
awn

born
borne
corn
dawn
fawn
forlorn
horn
lawn
morn
mourn
pawn
porn
scorn
Sean
shorn
stillborn
suborn
sworn
thorn
warn
worn
yawn

CORNER
fauna
fawner
Horner
Lorna
mourner
pawner
sauna
scorner
warner
yawner
(+ warn her *etc*)

CORNET
hornet
(+ pawn it *etc*)

ADORNING
awning
corning
dawning
fawning
morning
mourning
pawning
scorning
suborning
warning
yawning

BOROUGH
thorough

CORPSE
gawps
warps

TORRENT
abhorrent
torrent
warrant

HORRID
florid
forehead
horrid
quarried
torrid

ORRIS
Boris
Doris
Horace
lorris
Maurice
Morris

Norris
orris

BORROW
morrow
sorrow
tomorrow

LORRY
quarry
sorry

WORRY
see CURRY

HORSE
coarse
course
divorce
endorse
force
gorse
hoarse
horse
Morse
Norse
recourse
reinforce
remorse
resource
sauce
source

WORSE
see VERSE

WORST
see BURST

FORT
abort
aught
bought
brought
caught
cavort
contort
court
distort
escort
exhort
export
fort
fought
fraught
import
naught
nought
ought
port
quart
report
resort
retort
short
snort
sort
sought
sport
support
taught
taut
thought
thwart
tort
transport
wart
wrought

MORTAL
chortle

immortal
mortal
portal
(+ sport'll *etc*)

PORTER
daughter
exhorter
exporter
importer
porter
quarter
reporter
shorter
slaughter
snorter
sorter
supporter
tauter
thwarter
transporter
underwater
water
(+ brought a *etc*)

SHORTEST
tautest

FORTH
fourth
north

WORTH
see BIRTH

ABORTION
caution
contortion
distortion
portion
precaution
proportion

SHORTLY
courtly
portly
shortly
tautly

TORTURE
scorcher
torture
(+ debauch her *etc*)

TORTURED
orchard

FORTY
haughty
naughty
shorty
sortie
sporty
warty

DECORUM
forum
jorum
quorum
variorum
(+ bore 'em *etc*)

GLORY
gory
hoary
storey

story
Tory

AROSE
beaux
bestows
blows
bows
chose
close (verb & noun)
compose
crows
depose
disclose
dispose
doze
enclose
expose
floes
flows
foes
froze
glows
goes
grows
hellos
hoes
hose
impose
knows
lows
mows
noes
nose
oppose
outgrows
overflows
overthrows
owes
pose
propose
prose
repose
roes
rose
rows
sews
shows
sloes
slows
snows
sows
stows
suppose
those
throes
throws
toes
tows
transpose
undergoes
woes

DOSE
close (adj. & noun)
dose
gross
jocose
morose

LOSE
see AMUSE

EXPOSÉ
José
rosé

CLOSELY
grossly

jocosely
morosely

CH**OSEN**
frozen

CL**OSER**
grocer
grosser

CL**OSEST**
grossest

G**OSH**
nosh
posh
quash
slosh
splosh
squash
swash
tosh
wash

ACR**OSS**
boss
cross
doss
dross
emboss
fosse
gloss
joss
loss
moss
toss

GR**OSS**
see D**OSE**

B**OSSED**
accost
bossed
cost
crossed
dossed
embossed
frost
glossed
lost
tossed

F**OSSIL**
see AP**OSTLE**

P**OST**
boast
coast
dosed
ghost
grossed
host
most
oast
post
roast
toast

P**OSTER**
see B**OASTER**

C**OSTER**
foster
Gloucester
paternoster
roster
(+ lost her *etc*)

AP**OSTLE**
colossal
fossil
jostle

throstle
(+ boss'll *etc*)

GHOSTLY
mostly

COSY
dozy
nosy
posy
rosy

POT
allot
blot
clot
cot
dot
forgot
gavotte
got
hot
jot
knot
lot
not
plot
pot
rot
Scot
shot
slot
sot
spot
squat
swat
tot
trot
watt
what
yacht

ANECDOTAL
antidotal
sacerdotal
teetotal
total

BOTANY
cottony
monotony
(+ got any *etc*)

NOTCH
blotch
botch
crotch
notch
Scotch
watch

NOTE
afloat
bloat
boat
coat
denote
devote
dote
float
gloat
goat
groat
moat
note
oat
promote
quote
remote
rote

smote
stoat
throat
tote
vote
wrote

V**OTER**
bloater
boater
floater
motor
promoter
quota
remoter
rotor
voter

REM**OTEST**
noticed

BR**OTH**
cloth
froth
Goth
moth
wrath

B**OTH**
growth
loath
oath
sloth
troth

CL**OTHE**
betroth
clothe
loathe

AN**OTHER**
brother
mother
other
smother

CL**OTHES**
betroths
clothes
loathes
oaths

EM**OTION**
commotion
devotion
emotion
lotion
motion
notion
ocean
potion
promotion

EM**OTIONAL**
devotional
emotional
notional
promotional

PH**OTON**
proton
(+ coat on *etc*)

C**OTTAGE**
pottage
wattage

LOCOM**OTIVE**
motive
votive

ROTTEN
cotton
forgotten
gotten
rotten

BLOTTER
cotter
hotter
jotter
otter
plotter
potter
rotter
spotter
squatter
swatter
totter
trotter

LOTTERY
pottery
tottery

HOTTEST
squattest

BOTTLE
Aristotle
bottle
dottle
glottal
mottle
pottle
throttle
wattle

MOTTO
blotto
grotto
lotto
motto
risotto

DOUBLE
see BUBBLE

DOUBT
see ABOUT

COUCH
crouch
grouch
pouch
slouch
vouch

TOUCH
see CLUTCH

CROUCHER
sloucher
voucher

LOUD
see CROWD

LOUDER
see POWDER

LOUDEST
proudest

THOUGH
see BLOW

BOUGH
see NOW

ROUGH
see BLUFF

COUGH
see **OFF**

COUGHED
see AL**OFT**

BOUGHT
see F**ORT**

FOUL
see C**OWL**

SOUL
see H**OLE**

COULD
see G**OOD**

MOULD(ER)
see B**OLD(ER)**

NOUN
see BR**OWN**

ANNOUNCE
bounce
denounce
flounce
ounce
pounce
pronounce
renounce
trounce

ANNOUNCER
bouncer
denouncer
pronouncer
renouncer

AROUND
abound
aground
around
astound
bound
browned
clowned
compound
confound
crowned
drowned
expound
found
frowned
gowned
ground
hound
impound
mound
pound
profound
rebound
renowned
resound
round
sound
surround
wound

BOUNDER
compounder
expounder
flounder
founder
hounder
profounder
rounder
sounder

ROUNDEST
profoundest
roundest
soundest

BOUNDLESS
groundless
soundless

FOUNDLING
groundling

ROUNDLY
profoundly
roundly
soundly

YOUNG
see **BUNG**

ACCOUNT
amount
count
discount
dismount
fount
mount
recount
surmount

FOUNTAIN
mountain

BOUNTY
county
Mountie

SOUP
see **COOP**

TOUR
see **CURE**

HOUR
see **POWER**

DEVOURED
coward
cowered
devoured
flowered
glowered
Howard
loured
powered
scoured
showered
soured
towered

DEVOURER
flowerer
scourer
sourer

FLOURISH
nourish

HOURLY
sourly

ADJOURN
see **URN**

JOURNEY
attorney
Bernie
Ernie
journey

COURSE
see **HORSE**

COURSING
divorcing
endorsing
forcing
horsing
reinforcing
saucing

FOURTH
see **FORTH**

FLOURY
cowrie
dowry
floury
flowery
loury
showery

BLOUSE
allows
arouse
blouse
boughs
bows
brows
browse
carouse
chows
cows
dowse
drowse
house (verb)
endows
espouse
ploughs
prows
rouse
rows
soughs
sows
spouse
vows

MOUSE
douse
grouse
house (noun)
Laos
louse
mouse
nous
souse

COUSIN
dozen
cozen

OUST
doused
groused
joust
oust
roust
soused

ABOUT
bout
clout
devout
doubt
drought
flout
gout
knout
lout
nowt
out

pout
rout
scout
shout
snout
spout
sprout
stout
throughout
tout
trout
without

DEV**OUTER**
doubter
flouter
outer
pouter
scouter
shouter
spouter
stouter

DEV**OUTEST**
stoutest

M**OUTH**
drouth
mouth
south

OUTING
doubting
clouting
flouting
outing
pouting
routing
scouting
shouting
spouting
sprouting

APPR**OVAL**
disapproval
removal

AB**OVE**
dove
glove
guv
love
shove

CL**OVE**
cove
drove
grove
hove
Jove
mauve
rove
stove
strove
throve
wove

APPR**OVE**
disapprove
disprove
groove
improve
move
prove
remove
reprove

GR**OVEL**
hovel
novel

IMPR-
OVEMENT
movement

OVEN
coven
govern
oven
sloven

C**OVER**
discover
glover
lover
plover
recover
shover
uncover
undercover

CL**OVER**
Dover
drover
mauver
nova
over
rover

M**OVER**
Hoover
improver
manoeuvre
mover
Vancouver
(+ move her *etc*)

N**OW**
allow
bough
bow
brow
chow
cow
endow
how
now
plough
prow
row
Slough
sough
sow
vow

BL**OW**
ago
although
beau
below
bestow
blow
bow
crow
doe
dough
floe
flow
fro
glow
go
grow
hello
hoe
Joe
know
low
mow
no
outgrow
overflow
overthrow

owe
pro
roe
row
sew
show
sloe
slow
snow
so
sow
stow
though
throw
toe
tow
undergo
woe

COWARD
see DEV**OURED**

CROWD
allowed
aloud
bowed
cloud
cowed
crowd
endowed
loud
ploughed
proud
rowed
shroud
soughed
vowed

POWDER
chowder
louder
powder
prouder

SNOWED
see AB**ODE**

TOWEL
bowel
dowel
towel
trowel
vowel

POWER
bower
cower
devour
dower
flour
flower
glower
hour
lour
our
power
scour
shower
sour
tower

BLOWER
goer
grower
lower
mower
Noah
rower
sewer
slower

sower
thrower

P**OWERED**
see DEV**OURED**

L**OWEST**
slowest

B**OWL**
see H**OLE**

C**OWL**
foul
fowl
growl
howl
jowl
owl
prowl
scowl

ACKN-
OWLEDGE
college
knowledge

B**OWLER**
see CONTR**OLLER**

SL**OWLY**
holy
lowly
slowly
wholly

B**OWMAN**
foeman
omen
Roman
showman
yeoman

BR**OWN**
clown
crown
down
drown
frown
gown
noun
renown
town

BL**OWN**
see AL**ONE**

DR**OWNED**
see AR**OUND**

BR**OWNER**
crowner
downer
frowner

BL**OWS**
see AR**OSE**

BR**OWS(E)**
see BL**OUSE**

GR**OWTH**
see B**OTH**

BL**OWY**
Chloe
doughy
Joey
showy
snowy
Zoe

OX
see BL**OCKS**

D**OXY**
foxy
orthodoxy
proxy

T**OY**
ahoy
annoy
boy
buoy
cloy
coy
decoy
deploy
destroy
employ
enjoy
goy
joy
ploy
Roy
toy
Troy

L**OYAL**
see B**OIL**

L**OYALIST**
royalist

L**OYALLY**
royally

T**OYED**
annoyed
avoid
buoyed
cloyed
decoyed
deployed
destroyed
devoid
employed
enjoyed
Freud
joyed
Lloyd
toyed
void

EMPL**OYER**
coyer
employer
foyer
Goya
toyer

EMPL**OYMENT**
deployment
employment
enjoyment
unemployment

ANN**OYS**
boys
buoys
cloys
decoys
deploys
destroys
employs
enjoys
joys
noise
ploys
poise
toys

U

TR**UANT**
see FL**UENT**

CL**UB**
blub
chub
club
cub
drub
dub
grub
hub
nub
pub
rub
scrub
shrub
snub
stub
sub
tub

T**UBA**
Cuba
tuba
tuber

BL**UBBER**
clubber
grubber
lubber
rubber
scrubber
stubber
(+ snub her *etc*)

BL**UBBERED**
cupboard

B**UBBLE**
double
rubble
stubble
trouble
(+ pub'll *etc*)

C**UBE**
boob
cube
tube

PROD**UCE**
abstruse
abuse (noun)
Bruce
conduce
deduce
deuce
diffuse

disuse (noun)
excuse
goose
induce
introduce
juice
loose
moose
mousse
noose
obtuse
produce
profuse
puce
recluse
reduce
reproduce
seduce
sluice
spruce
traduce
truce
use (noun)

PROD**UCED**

boost
conduced
deduced
deuced
goosed
induced
introduced
loosed
noosed
produced
reduced
reproduced
seduced
sluiced
traduced
used

M**UCH**

see CL**UTCH**

D**UCK**

buck
chuck
cluck
duck
luck
muck
pluck
puck
ruck
shuck
struck
suck
truck
tuck

D**UCKED**

see COND**UCT**

S**UCKER**

chucker
chukker
mucker
pucker
succour
sucker
trucker
tucker

L**UCKIER**

pluckier

L**UCKIEST**

pluckiest

LUCKILY
pluckily

BUCKLE
chuckle
knuckle
suckle
truckle

DUCKS
bucks
chucks
clucks
crux
ducks
flux
plucks
pucks
rucks
shucks
sucks
trucks
tucks

LUCKY
ducky
Kentucky
mucky
plucky

CONDUCT
bucked
chucked
clucked
conduct
construct
deduct
ducked
duct
instruct
mucked
obstruct
plucked
product
reconstruct
rucked
shucked
sucked
trucked
tucked

DESTRUCTION
abduction
construction
deduction
destruction
fluxion
induction
instruction
introduction
obstruction
production
reduction
reproduction
ruction
seduction
suction

CONSTR-
UCTIVE
conductive
instructive
productive
reconstructive
seductive

CONSTR-
UCTIVELY
instructively
productively

reconstructively
seductively

MUD
blood
bud
cud
dud
flood
mud
scud
stud
sud
thud

RUDDER
shudder
udder

MUDDIER
bloodier
muddier
ruddier

MUDDIEST
bloodiest
muddiest
ruddiest

CUDDLE
fuddle
huddle
muddle
puddle
ruddle

MUDDY
bloody
buddy
muddy
ruddy
study

NUDE
allude
booed
brewed
brood
canoed
chewed
clued
conclude
crude
cued
delude
elude
endued
ensued
eschewed
exclude
exude
feud
food
glued
hewed
hued
imbued
include
interlude
intrude
Jude
lassooed
lewd
mewed
mooed
mood
nude
obtrude
protrude
prude

pursued
queued
renewed
reviewed
rued
rude
screwed
seclude
shampooed
shrewd
stewed
subdued
sued
tattooed
viewed
wooed

R**UDELY**
shrewdly
subduedly

PR**UDENT**
student

INTR**UDER**
Bermuda
brooder
intruder
lewder
nuder
ruder
shrewder

N**UDEST**
nudist
rudest
shrewdest

GR**UDGE**
budge
drudge
fudge
grudge
judge
misjudge
nudge
sludge
smudge
trudge

BL**UDGEON**
curmudgeon
dudgeon
gudgeon

CL**UE**
see DR**EW**

CR**UEL**
dual
duel
fuel
gruel
jewel
renewal

CR**UELLER**
dueller
jeweller

FL**UENT**
pursuant
truant

D**UES**
see AM**USE**

CR**UET**
suet
(+ do it *etc*)

BLUFF
buff
chough
chuff
cuff
duff
enough
fluff
gruff
guff
huff
luff
muff
puff
rebuff
rough
ruff
slough
snuff
stuff
tough

BLUFFED
buffed
chuffed
cuffed
huffed
luffed
muffed
puffed
rebuffed
roughed
ruffed
sloughed
snuffed
stuffed
tuft

BLUFFER
buffer
duffer
gruffer
puffer
rougher
snuffer
stuffer
suffer
tougher

BLUFFEST
gruffest
roughest
toughest

BUFFET
tuffet
(+ rough it *etc*)

MUFFIN
puffin

RUFFLE
duffel
duffle
kerfuffle
muffle
ruffle
scuffle
shuffle
snuffle
truffle

MUFFLER
shuffler
snuffler

BLUFFLY
gruffly
roughly
toughly

FLUFFY
huffy
puffy
stuffy

TUFT
see BLUFFED

BUG
chug
drug
dug
fug
glug
hug
jug
lug
mug
plug
pug
rug
shrug
slug
smug
snug
thug
trug
tug

HUGE
Scrooge
stooge

MUGGER
bugger
lugger
rugger
smugger
snugger

JUGGLE
smuggle
snuggle
struggle

SNUGLY
smugly
ugly

JUICE
see PRODUCE

BUILDER
see BEWILDER

BUILDING
gilding

BUILT
see HILT

ENQUIRY
see DIARY

FRUIT
see CUTE

DUKE
fluke
Luke
puke
rebuke
snook
spook
stook

GULCH
mulch

RULE(R)
see COOL(ER)

BULGE
divulge
indulge

BULK
hulk
skulk
sulk

BULKY
sulky

BULL
full
pull
wool

DULL
annul
cull
dull
gull
hull
lull
mull
null
scull
skull

DULLER
colour
culler
duller
sculler

BULLY
fully
pulley
woolly

DULLY
gully
sully

GULP
pulp

PULSE
convulse
impulse
pulse
repulse

CULT
adult
consult
cult
exult
insult
occult
result

AGRIC-ULTURAL
cultural
horticultural

CULTURE
vulture

DULY
see COOLLY

DRUM
become
bum
chum

come
crumb
drum
dumb
glum
gum
hum
mum
numb
overcome
plum
plumb
rum
scrum
scum
slum
some
strum
succumb
sum
swum
thrum
thumb

L**UMBER**
encumber
Humber
lumbar
lumber
number
rumba
slumber

D**UMBEST**
glummest
numbest
rummest

F**UMBLE**
bumble
crumble
fumble
grumble
humble
jumble
mumble
rumble
scumble
stumble
tumble
umbel

F**UMBLER**
grumbler
humbler
mumbler
stumbler
tumbler

ASS**UME**
bloom
boom
broom
consume
doom
exhume
fume
gloom
groom
loom
perfume
plume
presume
resume
rheum
room
spume
tomb
whom
womb
zoom

LUMINOUS
bituminous
leguminous
luminous
numinous
voluminous

LUMINOUSLY
voluminously

DRUMMER
dumber
glummer
hummer
mummer
number
plumber
summer

DRUMMING
becoming
coming
drumming
gumming
humming
mumming
numbing
overcoming
plumbing
slumming
strumming
succumbing
summing
thrumming
thumbing

SUMMIT
grummet
plummet
summit
(+ hum it *etc*)

MUMMY
crumby
dummy
lumme
mummy
plummy
rummy
scummy
tummy
yummy

HUMOROUS
humerus
numerous
tumorous

HUMOROUSLY
numerously

HUMOUR
bloomer
consumer
humour
rumour
tumour

BUMP
chump
clump
dump
frump
hump
jump
lump
plump
pump
rump
slump

stump
sump
thump
trump

BUMPER
dumper
jumper
plumper
stumper
thumper

CRUMPET
strumpet
trumpet
(+ bump it *etc*)

BUMPY
dumpy
frumpy
grumpy
jumpy
lumpy
stumpy

BUN
begun
bun
done
dun
fun
gun
hun
none
nun
one
pun
run
shun
son
spun
stun
sun
ton
tun
undone
won

DUNCE
affronts
blunts
bunts
confronts
dunce
fronts
grunts
hunts
once
punts
runts
shunts
stunts

BUNCH
brunch
bunch
crunch
hunch
lunch
munch
punch
scrunch

LUNCHEON
puncheon
truncheon

DEFUNCT
bunked
clunked
defunct

disjunct
dunked
flunked
funked

FUNCTION
compunction
junction
unction

FUND
gunned
punned
rotund
shunned
stunned
sunned

ABUNDANT
redundant

ABUNDANTLY
redundantly

BLUNDER
chunder
plunder
sunder
thunder
under
wonder

BLUNDERER
plunderer
thunderer
wonderer

BUNDLE
trundle

PRUNE
see AFTERNOON

BUNG
among
bung
clung
dung
flung
hung
lung
rung
slung
sprung
strung
stung
sung
swung
tongue
wrung
young

PLUNGE
expunge
gunge
lunge
plunge
sponge

HUNGER
fishmonger
hunger
ironmonger
younger

PLUNGER
conjure
lunger
plunger
sponger

BUNGLE
jungle

BUNION
Bunyan
onion
trunnion

COMMUNITY
immunity
importunity
impunity
opportunity
unity

BUNK
chunk
clunk
drunk
dunk
flunk
funk
hunk
junk
monk
punk
shrunk
skunk
slunk
spunk
stunk
sunk
trunk

BUNKER
drunker
hunker

FUNNEL
gunwale
runnel
tunnel

GUNNER
runner
shunner
stunner

FUNNIER
runnier
sunnier

FUNNIEST
runniest
sunniest

CUNNING
dunning
gunning
punning
running
shunning
stunning
sunning

FUNNY
bunny
funny
gunny
honey
money
runny
sunny
tunny

BLUNT
affront
blunt
brunt

bunt
confront
front
grunt
hunt
punt
runt
shunt
stunt

BL**UNTER**
grunter
hunter
punter

BL**UNTING**
affronting
blunting
bunting
confronting
fronting
grunting
hunting
punting
shunting
stunting

BL**UNTS**
see D**UNCE**

C**UP**
pup
sup
tup
up

S**UPPER**
crupper
cuppa
scupper
supper
upper

ABR**UPT**
corrupt
cupped
disrupt
erupt
interrupt
supped
tupped
upped

C**UR**
aver
blur
burr
concur
cur
defer
deter
err
fir
fur
her
infer
myrrh
occur
per
prefer
purr
recur
refer
sir
slur
spur
stir
transfer
were
whirr

CURABLE
durable
endurable
incurable
insurable
procurable

PLURAL
mural
plural
rural

ASSURANCE
durance
endurance
insurance
reassurance

DISTURB
blurb
curb
disturb
herb
kerb
perturb
superb
verb

TURBAN
suburban
turban
urban

BURBOT
Herbert
sherbet
turbot

CHURCH
besmirch
birch
church
lurch
perch
research
search
smirch

LURCHER
nurture
researcher
searcher

ABSURD
averred
bird
concurred
curd
deferred
deterred
erred
furred
gird
heard
herd
inferred
occurred
preferred
purred
recurred
referred
sherd
slurred
spurred
stirred
third
transferred
whirred
word

ABSURDER
girder

herder
murder

CURDLE
girdle
hurdle

CURE
allure
assure
boor
cure
demure
endure
ensure
epicure
ewer
hewer
immature
insure
liqueur
lure
manure
mature
moor
obscure
poor
premature
procure
pure
reassure
secure
skewer
sure
tour
you're
(Some of these words have an alternative pronunciation rhyming with ADORE.)

PURELY
demurely
immaturely
maturely
obscurely
poorly
prematurely
purely
securely
surely

PURER
demurer
immaturer
insurer
maturer
obscurer
poorer
purer
securer
surer
tourer

PUREST
demurest
immaturest
jurist
maturest
obscurest
poorest
purest
purist
securest
surest
tourist

TURF
scurf

serf
surf
turf

URGE
converge
dirge
diverge
emerge
merge
purge
scourge
serge
splurge
spurge
submerge
surge
urge
verge

URGENT
detergent
divergent
emergent
resurgent
urgent

B**URGEON**
sturgeon
surgeon

S**URGERY**
see PERJURY

B**URGLE**
gurgle

C**URIOUS**
furious
injurious
luxurious
penurious
spurious

P**URITY**
immaturity
maturity
obscurity
purity
security

L**URK**
burk
burke
dirk
irk
jerk
kirk
lurk
murk
perk
quirk
shirk
smirk
Turk
work

L**URKER**
Gurkha
jerker
lurker
shirker
smirker
worker
(+ irk her *etc*)

M**URKY**
jerky
murky
perky
quirky

CURL
churl
curl
earl
furl
girl
hurl
pearl
purl
swirl
twirl
whirl

CURLED
furled
hurled
pearled
purled
swirled
twirled
whirled
world

CURLIER
burlier
curlier
earlier
surlier

CURLIEST
burliest
curliest
earliest
surliest

CURLINESS
burliness
curliness
earliness
surliness

CURLY
burly
curly
early
girlie
hurly-burly
pearly
Shirley
surly
whirly

URN
adjourn
burn
churn
concern
discern
earn
fern
learn
overturn
quern
return
spurn
stern
turn
urn
yearn

BURNER
earner
learner
returner
sterner
turner
yearner

BURNISH
furnish

BURP
chirp
twirp
usurp

BURROW
furrow

CURRY
flurry
hurry
Murray
scurry
slurry
Surrey
worry

CURSE
see VERSE

BURST
coerced
conversed
cursed
dispersed
durst
first
headfirst
immersed
nursed
pursed
rehearsed
reimbursed
reversed
thirst
traversed
worst

BLURT
see ALERT

CURTAIN
see CERTAIN

CURVE
see SERVE

FURY
Jewry
jury
Missouri

BURY
see BERRY

BUS
buss
cuss
discuss
fuss
huss
muss
plus
pus
suss
thus
truss
us

MUSCLE
see BUSTLE

AMUSE
abuse
accuse
amuse
bamboos
blues
booze

brews
bruise
canoes
chews
choose
clues
confuse
crews
cruise
dews
dues
excuse
fuse
glues
jews
kangaroos
lassos
lose
mews
misuse
moos
muse
news
ooze
peruse
pews
pursues
queues
refuse
renews
reviews
ruse
screws
shampoos
shoes
stews
subdues
sues
suffuse
taboos
tattoos
transfuse
use
views
whose
zoos

PROF**USE**

see PROD**UCE**

USER

accuser
boozer
bruiser
chooser
cruiser
loser
refuser
user

BL**USH**

brush
crush
flush
gush
hush
lush
mush
plush
rush
slush
thrush
tush

B**USH**

push

BL**USHER**

brusher
crusher
gusher

lusher
plusher
Prussia
rusher
Russia
usher

LUSHEST
plushest

CONCLUSION
confusion
contusion
delusion
fusion
illusion

DUSK
brusque
busk
dusk
husk
musk
rusk
tusk

FUSS
see BUS

CONCUSSION
discussion
percussion
Prussian
repercussion
Russian

ADJUST
august
bused
bussed
bust
crust
cussed
discussed
disgust
distrust
dust
entrust
fussed
gust
just
lust
mistrust
mussed
must
nonplussed
robust
rust
sussed
thrust
trust
trussed

CUSTARD
blustered
bustard
clustered
custard
flustered
lustred
mustard
mustered

ADJUSTER
auguster
bluster
buster
cluster
duster
fluster

juster
lustre
muster
robuster
thruster

ADJ**USTING**
busting
crusting
disgusting
distrusting
dusting
entrusting
gusting
husting
lusting
mistrusting
rusting
thrusting
trusting

B**USTLE**
corpuscle
hustle
muscle
rustle
tussle

AUG**USTLY**
justly
robustly

ACC**USTOM**
custom
frustum

D**USTY**
busty
crusty
dusty
fusty
gusty
lusty
musty
rusty
trusty

B**USY**
see D**IZZY**

B**UT**
butt
cut
glut
gut
hut
jut
mutt
nut
putt
rebut
rut
scut
shut
slut
smut
strut
tut

P**UT**
see F**OOT**

INSCR**UTABLE**
commutable
confutable
dilutable
disputable
executable
imputable
persecutable
prosecutable
recruitable

refutable
substitutable
suitable
transmutable

CLUTCH

crutch
Dutch
hutch
much
smutch
such
touch

CUTE

absolute
acute
astute
attribute
boot
brute
cheroot
chute
commute
compute
confute
contribute
coot
cute
destitute
dilute
dispute
dissolute
distribute
electrocute
execute
fruit
hoot
impute
institute
jute
loot
lute
minute
moot
mute
newt
persecute
pollute
prosecute
prostitute
pursuit
recruit
refute
repute
resolute
root
route
salute
scoot
shoot
substitute
suit
toot
transmute

CUTER

acuter
astuter
commuter
computer
confuter
cuter
diluter
disputer
hooter
looter
minuter
muter
neuter
persecutor

polluter
prosecutor
recruiter
refuter
scooter
shooter
suitor
tutor

TR**UTH**
see TOOTH

D**UTIFUL**
beautiful

M**UTINY**
scrutiny

CONSTIT**UTION**
absolution
attribution
constitution
contribution
destitution
devolution
distribution
electrocution
elocution
evolution
execution
institution
persecution
pollution
prosecution
prostitution
resolution
restitution
revolution
solution
substitution

B**UTTER**
clutter
cutter
flutter
gutter
mutter
nutter
putter
shutter
splutter
sputter
strutter
stutter
utter

B**UTTON**
glutton
Hutton
mutton
Sutton

B**UTTY**
nutty
putty
smutty

D**UTY**
beauty
booty
duty
fruity
snooty

CR**UX**
see DUCKS